We dedicate these pages
to the memories of
the men and women of Belfast
who have left us a legacy to honor and
cherish.

# Table of Contents

❧

# The Past is Before Us

❧

Collected readings from the first
twenty-five years of the Belfast Historical
Society newsletter "The Recaller".

Edited by
Eliza Gillis
Viola Gillis
Linda Jean Nicholson MacKenzie

❧

Published by
The Belfast Historical Society

*Printing*
Williams and Crue

*Front Cover*. Gravestone of Alexander Nicholson, a native of the Isle of Skye, who died in 1820. Located at the "Old French Cemetery" near Selkirk Park, Belfast. [Photo courtesy of L. J. N. MacKenzie.]

The book was published with financial assistance from the Province of Prince Edward Island Cultural Development Program, Department of Community and Cultural Affairs.

**Canadian Cataloguing in Publication Data**

The past is before us: collected readings from the first twenty-five years of the Belfast Historical Society newsletter "The recaller" / edited by Eliza Gillis, Viola Gillis, Linda Jean Nicholson MacKenzie.

Includes bibliographical references and index.
ISBN 0-9685586-0-7

1. Belfast (P.E.I.)--History.  2. Belfast (P.E.I.)--Biography.  3. Belfast (P.E.I.)--Anecdotes.  I. Gillis, Eliza,  II. Gillis, Viola,  III. MacKenzie, Linda Jean Nicholson,  IV. Belfast Historical Society (P.E.I.)

FC2649.B43P37 2002          971.7'4          C2002-904767-6
F1049.5.B43P37 2002

# Chapter Three: Schools

# Chapter Four: Businesses

# Chapter Five: Community Service

## Chapter Six: The Sea

## Chapter Seven: Military Service

## Chapter Eight: Progress

# Acknowledgements

❧

A book such as this requires assistance from many individuals. We want to thank all those who were kind enough to lend us their photographs and memorabilia. We wanted to publish all of them. Unfortunately, due to space and time limitations, we were unable to use many of the photographs given to us.

We would also like to thank those who took the time to furnish us with invaluable information about people, places and events.

In particular, this book would not have been possible without the kind assistance of: Ruth Acorn, Miriam Bell, Elizabeth Boehner, Alan Buchanan, Jean Cantelo, Donna Collings, Bertie Cook, Helen Crocker, George and Helen Docherty, Layton Docherty, Suzanne Dornbach, Mary Dugas, Margaret Edmonds, Norma Enman, Catherine Fraser, Donald Garnhum, Elinor Gillis, Lauchlin Gillis, Leonard Grierson, Edna Halliday, Gladys Hancock, Howard and Frances Hancock, Dave Hunter, Joyce Kennedy, Kaye Kennedy, Donna Knox, Marion Finlayson, Kenny and Phyllis McCabe, Brenda MacDonald, Isabel MacDonald, Janice MacDonald, Mary MacEachern, Auldene MacKenzie, Donald MacKenzie, John MacKenzie, Tommy and Dora MacKenzie, Blair MacKinnon, Willena MacKinnon, Jean MacLean, Johnny and Marie MacLean, Malcolm MacLean, Edna and Ernest MacLeod, Alan MacMillan, Ann MacPherson, Josephine MacPherson, Marion MacRae, Stewart and Barbara MacRae, Sinclair and Thelma MacTavish, Edith Martin, Clarence Moore, Thelma Murchison, Esther Mutch, Keith Nicholson, Florence O'Shea, Margaret Panton, Peggy and Billy Penny, Charlotte Ross, Mary Ross, and Jean Stewart. Also Kevin MacDonald and Charlotte Stewart from the Public Archives, St. Andrew's United Church, and Hillcrest United Church.

And finally, we would like to thank our families and husbands for their patience and support while we worked on this most important project.

# Introduction

☙❧

At the Founding Meeting of the Belfast Historical Society in March of 1976, newly elected President Harry Baglole suggested the Society publish a quarterly newsletter. Soon after, the Executive Committee approved a motion to establish *The Recaller* as the newsletter of the Belfast Historical Society.

The first issue of *The Recaller* was four pages in length and contained several current event notices, two local history articles, and an article about the creation of the Belfast Historical Society. In subsequent issues, articles published in *The Recaller* would cover a wide range of subjects, many celebrating the history, activities, and people of Belfast.

As part of the 200th Anniversary celebrating the arrival of the Selkirk Settlers, it was decided that a committee would be formed and given the task of creating a book from the hundreds of articles published in the first twenty-five years of *The Recaller* newsletter. The present Editors were asked to become that committee.

During our first meetings, we selected a basic criteria which all articles had to meet for inclusion in the book. Most importantly, we chose to include only those articles written about people, places or events in or near Belfast.

Once we selected our first "pool" of articles, we had to organize them into chapters, and search for accompanying photographs and memorabilia. The next step was the most difficult – editing and cutting articles. Space became a problem, as we had too many pages and we spent a great deal of time struggling with the decisions of selecting articles. In the end our decisions were based on what we believed would serve best for the book.

This book is not a complete history of the Belfast area. It might best be described as an album containing snapshots of places, people, and events occurring at various times in Belfast. Our objective was to present these diverse articles in a way that is appealing to the reader, yet respects the original work. We hope we have succeeded.

Eliza Gillis
Viola Gillis
Linda J. N. MacKenzie
Editors

## *Chapter One*

### ❦

# *Our Early History*

"The past is a priceless heritage and the story of fortitude and faith during the years of trial in the wilderness of Belfast should not be forgotten."

– Malcolm MacQueen, *Hebridean Pioneers*.

The Selkirk Settlement Monument at Selkirk Park, Eldon: "The settlement founded in this area by Thomas Douglas, Fifth Earl of Selkirk, was the first systematic attempt to direct to British North America the tide of dispossessed Highlanders which had been flowing to industrial Britain and the United States. The 800 settlers who arrived here in 1803 aboard the *Polly*, *Dykes*, and *Oughton* enjoyed Selkirk's financial support and personal supervision, and settled on land which he had purchased. Together with earlier immigrants from the Highlands and Hebrides, the Selkirk Settlers established an enduring Scottish tradition in Prince Edward Island." Erected by the Historic Sites and Monuments Board of Canada.

# The Ship *Polly*

## Letters from Basil Greenhill

In a letter dated 7 July 1976, Basil Greenhill, Director of the National Maritime Museum in England responded to a request from Harry Baglole, President of the Belfast Historical Society for detailed information about the ship *Polly* . The *Polly* had been one of three vessels engaged in 1803 by Lord Selkirk to transport passengers to the Belfast District of Prince Edward Island. Following is an excerpt from Mr. Greenhill's letter:

"Thank you for your letter of June 9, which incidentally has been useful in assisting us to identify the *Polly* positively among the several ships of that name on the register. We have been able to be sure that she was a shiprigged vessel built at Whitby in 1762 and rebuilt there in 1798. In these circumstances, she was clearly a similar vessel, though slightly smaller, to those used by Captain Cook, of which good plans exist, as well as resembling the cat bark of which we have a very good model, an illustration of which I enclose. I will arrange for you to be sent copies of the plans of the *Endeavor* and this material should suffice to enable you to produce a good model. At a later stage, I shall also send a record of the *Polly* as extracted from the registers of the time so that you will have all the available information about her."

In a second letter, dated 21 July 1976, Mr. Greenhill supplied additional information about the ship:

"The *Polly*, which took the early settlers to Prince Edward Island, was a ship of 281 tons. . .she is described in her British Registration material as having a single deck and her draught was 15 feet. She was sheathed in 1800. Her original owner was named Broderick and her master was W. Blackburn. In 1799, she was voyaging to Hamburg. The same year she was sold to Darby and Co. of London, and traded to the West Indies, under Captain T. Darby.[1] In 1803, she made the voyage to Prince Edward Island, but otherwise appears to have traded to Jamaica until in 1806, she was sold to Henley and Co. of London and employed largely as a transport under Captain Chapman, and from 1812 Captain Pringle, and in 1815 Captain Edwards.

In 1818, she was re-rigged as a brig and continued with Henleys in the Baltic and North American trades, until 1824, when she was sold to Kane and Son for the Archangel trade, and the following year, disappears from the Register."

[The letter dated 21 July 1976 was published in *The Recaller*, November 1997.]

[1]According to Lucille Campey in *A Very Fine Class of Immigrants*, the owner (Darby and Co.) and Captain (T. Darby) were one and the same.

# Where the *Polly* Passengers Landed

*Prince Edward Island Magazine*, August 1904.

By the kindness of Mr. D. A. McDonald of Eldon, we are enabled to give some particulars of the landing place of the passengers by the famous ship *Polly*, which brought out many of the Lord Selkirk settlers to Belfast, P.E.I. in 1803. The land where the settlers stepped ashore was first acquired by a Captain McMillan, who procured it from Lord Selkirk in 1823. It came into the possession of Captain McMillan's son in 1825. His son, Alexander McMillan, now of Eldon, informs us that the property was disposed of to Mr. D. A. McDonald's father, the late John S. McDonald. A small portion of the land near the shore was owned for a time by a man named Gillis. The late Mr. McDonald purchased this also, and his heirs, at present, possess all the land contiguous to the landing place.

The Mr. Gillis referred to above was the uncle of Rev. John Gillis, who some time ago lived in Dundas, Kings Co. The grandparents of the revered gentleman lived quite close to the French graveyard – which formerly occupied a site near the landing place – up to the time of their grandfather's death when they all moved away.

A building was erected by the settlers, near to this Old French Burial ground, which was used for church service. The late Charles McKinnon, the grandfather of the present Mr. McDonald was the first local preacher.

A number of the immigrants were buried in the Old French Graveyard: the McTavishes, Martins, McPhees, Nicholsons, Dochertys, and many others.

[Published in *The Recaller*, April 2000. Editors Note: There are several conflicting views regarding the exact landing place of the *Polly* passengers. In his diary, Lord Selkirk made the following entry upon his arrival in Belfast on August 13th, "I found the people scattered about along a mile of Shore . . . in hovels or wigwams." The *Polly* was anchored in Orwell Bay and from Selkirk's description, it is likely the settlers landed in several locations along the shore, not one location.]

---

"Pioneering imposes heavy toil on women. In addition to providing clothing for the whole family they assisted at haying and harvest, for these crops were always menaced by heavy rain and winds. In every home a spinning wheel was as conspicuous a part of the household furniture as the bedstead, and in many homes there was a loom. Spinning and weaving through long hours, the women beguiled away the time humming or singing well known Scottish ballads, or even psalms."

- Malcolm MacQueen, *Hebridean Pioneers*.

# The Polly Spring
*Hugh MacDonald*

Scottish immigrants from the ship *Polly* which set anchor in Martin's Cove, Belfast on August 7, 1803, immediately hiked up along Martin's Creek in search of fresh water. About half a mile from its mouth, they discovered a beautiful spring draining into the creek. Fresh water on the *Polly* was perhaps quite adequate in supply, but must have been getting stale after so many weeks at sea. It is safe to say that all immigrants quickly partook of the cool fresh water of "Polly Spring", as it was named. This must have tended to counter the pessimism and softened the discouragement that many must have felt after so long a voyage, and having to face a seemingly inhospitable land – a land which had been going back to nature since the expulsion of the Acadians 45 years earlier.

From a newspaper article a hundred years ago, we learn that –

> "Many were those who sighed
> 'Oh, why left I my home? Why did I cross the deep?
> Oh, why left I the land where my forefathers sleep?
> I sigh for Scotia's shore, and I gaze across the sea,
> But, I cannot get a blink o' my ain country.'"

With the removal of trees, and perhaps for other reasons, springs and creeks, which once flowed swiftly to the sea, are now reduced to little more than a trickle. However, the Polly Spring can still provide the passerby with delicious cool water. It is situated about 150 yards west of the Trans Canada Highway, and 400 yards south of the road leading to the Selkirk Park.

[Published in *The Recaller*, Autumn 1978.]

---

# Who Was She?
*Janet Dale*

She had "red hair and thick lips" according to some observant citizens of the Belfast area in 1815, and she went by the name of Mary Halliday. But, there is no doubt that she was not born a Halliday for her guardian Thomas Halliday, made this clear in a letter he wrote to the Earl of Selkirk in the same year. In that letter, a copy of which is in the possession of the Belfast Historical Society, Halliday disclosed that "she goes under the name of Mary Halliday by her own wish for she thinks it more honorable to belong to the family than not."

Mary Cochrane had been placed in the care of the Halliday family of Edinburgh by the time she was ten years old. In return for raising her, the Hallidays were to be given free land on Prince Edward Island by Thomas Douglas, Earl of Selkirk. Mary was also to receive a tract of free land, separate from that of the Hallidays.

Hindered by an uncooperative land agent, the Hallidays did not actually obtain the land, first promised to them in 1809, until close to 1820. Mary married Thomas Halliday, Jr., son of her guardian.

What was Mary's relationship to the Earl of Selkirk, who had in 1807 married a Scottish woman, Jean Wedderburn, but who had taken such pains to provide for little Mary Halliday? Many Belfast residents, among them Mary's own daughter, Ellen Halliday MacLellan (or MacLennan) believed that Mary was Lord Selkirk's own daughter from a relationship that had preceded his marriage.

Selkirk died in 1819 and Mary in 1859 - perhaps taking with them the secret of Mary's identity. The stone in St. John's Presbyterian Cemetery refers to

In loving
Memory of
MARY DOUGLAS
only daughter of
Lord Selkirk
DIED
OCT 1859
Æt. 60

E. McLennan

sketch by
Michael Shumate

**Gravestone of Mary Cochrane Douglas at St. John's Presbyterian Church Cemetery, Belfast.**
The bottom lines on the stone read, "Blessed are the dead who die in the Lord." and "Erected by her daughter E. McLennan".

Mary as neither Mary Halliday nor Mary Cochrane, but as Mary Douglas, "only daughter of the Earl of Selkirk." In fact, Selkirk and his wife Jean had two daughters and a son.

The mystery of Mary remains unsolved.

[Published in *The Recaller*, Autumn 1976. Editors Note: For additional information on the mysterious origins of Mary Halliday, see *The Island Magazine*, Spring/Summer 1986, "Thomas Halliday, Mary Cochrane, the Earl of Selkirk, and the Island", Introduced and Annotated by J. M. Bumsted.]

# Dr. Angus McAulay

*Linda Jean Nicholson MacKenzie*

Among the passengers who arrived in Belfast in 1803 on the ship *Polly* was Angus McAulay, a minister and medical doctor. As agent for Lord Selkirk, Dr. McAulay had inspired many of his countrymen to join him in immigrating to Prince Edward Island as part of the group that would later be know as the "Selkirk Settlers".

**Dr. Angus McAulay. A posthumous portrait painted by Robert Harris, ca. 1870.**
[Prince Edward Island Public Archives and Records Office, Accession 3753, Item 11.]

Dr. McAulay was held in great esteem by his fellow settlers, and his loyalty to them was undiminished by any fears of offending the ruling gentry of the Island. He publicly spoke his mind and often defended those in less advantageous positions than himself.

One example of Dr. McAulay's outspoken nature is found in a letter he had written to a London newspaper in hopes of discouraging settlers. The letter was republished in the Charlottetown *Weekly Recorder* on March 16, 1811: "September 20th, Charlottetown, Prince Edward Island.

We have four, out of five vessels from Scotland, with emigrants already arrived, and for the sake of humanity, I hope the fifth may not --- as independent of the late period at which they must arrive if they do come, the scantiness of our crops arising from a long continuation of hot and dry weather will render it a very difficult matter for them to make out sufficient sustenance for the winter. --- In short it is a most infamous traffick in the way it is carried on. The poor ignorant wretches are deluded by false and exaggerated accounts of the Island to quit perhaps comfortable situations at home and come here paying for the least children £10 sterling, and such as have not the money to pay down are induced to give their obligation (notes) payable on demand, which have been put into the hands of an Attorney the day after they have landed; and those who have no friends to advance the money or to go bail for them, are cast into Prison, tho' they declare that they were Solemnly promised they should not be called on until it was perfectly convenient for them to pay. Add to this they are turned out on a BEACH without a place to shelter themselves in, except an old Windmill, which is used by Government as a Telegraph, and is pervious to every blast."

The editor of the Charlottetown *Weekly Recorder* added the following note: "As it has been the theme of much public conversation for some days past, without being seen by very few, we publish it for the satisfaction of our readers . . . this letter is the production of Doctor McAulay, Justice of the Peace, who it appears has been active in collecting information in his head. In it, he pledges himself to adduce proof to what he asserts as facts, in vindication of the extract in *The Chronicle*, and proceeds in a commendable manner to state the friendly and hospitable treatment those people met on their arrival, not only by individuals and people of different classes, but by the colony's highest source of patronage. These facts which are well known to every individual who have resided for any time within the limits of this town. In noticing the benevolence which is stated in Doctor MacAulay's letter, and which is generally known to have been evinced, to the poor people who have, from perhaps a too flowery description of the country, been induced to come to it . . ."

Dr. McAulay would later represent the people of Queens County in the Legislative Assembly and would twice fill the Speakers chair. He died on December 6, 1827. His death notice, published in the *PEI Register*, gave this appropriate effigy: "Whatever opinion may be entertained of the soundness of his views, or the judiciousness of his conduct as a public man, we believe it will be conceded, even by his adversaries, that at heart he was sincerely desirous of promoting the prosperity of the country. The poor in the neighbourhood where he lived, have in him lost a sincere benefactor whom they will long remember with gratitude."

[Published in *The Recaller*, April 2001.]

# A Century Ago

*Hugh MacDonald*

Over a century ago things were very different. As soon as a place was cleared for a log cabin, the early pioneers made arrangements for a place to meet together and worship and for a place where children could come together to learn.

In 1769, the population of Prince Edward Island was 271. But by 1861, the census shows the population had increased to 81,000, with 156 churches and 300 schools.

One hundred years ago people knew little of modern medicine, but they had many good home remedies. On account of their rugged outdoor life, they grew strong. Doctors would be sent for only in cases of emergency. The doctors too endured hardships, and travelling long distances on horseback.

There was respect for the Sabbath, when only necessary farm work and house work was done. Many walked miles to places of worship, not only on Sunday, but also on prayer meeting nights. Some came with horse and coach over rough roads and corduroy roads, where poles were laid across marshy places. Most homes had a Bible and it was read daily.

In some Scottish settlements, church services were given in both English and Gaelic. The church choir consisted of men and the singing was led by a presenter. People were known to walk from Strathalbyn to Valleyfield to attend summer Communion services. The parish of a minister or priest took in a large area and all were untiring and faithful in ministering to the spiritual needs of their respective people and with small monetary remuneration. Money was scarce, and collections in churches consisted mainly of large coppers.

In school, the three "R's" (reading, writing and arithmetic) were the chief subjects of importance. Before 1864 schools were not very good and attendance was irregular, but after this time there was a marked improvement. Prince of Wales College and St. Dunstan's College were established and enrollments in each rural school increased to about forty. The majority of teachers were male. In some schools there were both desks and the earlier-used long benches. Slates and slate pencils were used. Children learned Gaelic at home. But at school, it was a common rule that anyone heard to speak Gaelic would be punished.

From the rural schools of that era have come outstanding teachers, clergymen, doctors, lawyers, politicians, and many others distinguished at home and abroad.

[Published in *The Recaller*, September 1993.]

# The Irish in Belfast

*Father Arthur O'Shea*

[Condensed from a speech given by Father O'Shea on June 28, 1990 at the Iona Hall.]

Motivated by the difficulties of raising large families in a poor country, by political persecution, and by a spirit of adventure, the Irish pioneers left their homeland. Most were from the southeast counties of Ireland, with the last group coming from the northern counties. These Irish immigrants arrived between 1827 and 1842, and it is significant that they all came prior to the Great Famine, as they were poor, but not destitute. In 1841, the Census of Prince Edward Island listed 157 Irish natives residing in Iona and Newtown.

**St. Michael's Roman Catholic Church, Iona.** [Photo courtesy of L. J. N. MacKenzie.]

The name "Iona" was given to the community in 1901. It was named for Iona Island located off the west coast of Scotland where St. Columba had established a missionary centre dating from the 6th century AD. In 1905, the railway station in Iona was named "Fodhla", a poetic name for Ireland.

Construction on the first church began in 1850, prior to which the house of Martin Daley was a Mass station. The church had a 92 foot spire and a gallery that ran around three sides of the sanctuary. On January 1, 1926, it burned to the ground.

The second church, built on the same site, was a larger edifice. But, it was never completed, due to the onset of the Great Depression, which was followed by the demands of wartime. On January 6, 1959 the church burst into flames.

The third, and present church, stands on the same site. But, while it runs east and west, as had the first structure, the main door is on the opposite side (i.e. on the upper side).  The second building had run north and south.

There was a resident priest in Iona for 102 years.  At least twelve boys who had attended school in Iona became priests, and six of those remained in Prince Edward Island.

The parish hall was built in 1914.  It has been used for plays, suppers, debates, and political meetings.  In 1926 and again in 1959, the hall was used as a church, while rebuilding was being carried out.

There were several outstanding persons in the history of Iona.  These included Patrick Stevens, Father James Phelan, James Daly, Pat Bolger, and Joe Farrell.

[Published in *The Recaller*, October 1990.]

---

# In His Own Words

*Linda Jean Nicholson MacKenzie*

In the early 1800's, it was common for an individual making an affidavit to supply biographical information before giving evidence. Affidavits were made under oath, a factor which substantially increases their value to the family historian.  A good example of deponents offering personal information in affidavits appears in the Chancery Court case, "John Doe on the demise of Andrew Colville, Adam Mailland and John Hacket, Plaintiffs v. Lauchlan MacLean, Defendant", 1851.  The deponents in this case were all early residents of Belfast.  Below are abstracts from their affidavits.

"*John Buchanan* of Township Number 24, farmer, maketh oath and saith that he settled in Belfast in or about the year 1803, having come to this Colony in the Ship *Polly* and resided at Belfast until in or about the year 1837."                                          Sworn on May 1, 1852.

"*Donald Buchanan* of Township 57, Farmer . . . saith that he is 57 years of age, to the best of his belief, and a son of Malcolm Buchanan late of Portage, Belfast, deceased.  This deponent saith that his late brother Duncan Buchanan had agreed to purchase 100 acres of land from the late Earl of Selkirk to be paid for in labour, but having very soon thereafter been accidentally killed, the said Earl of Selkirk agreed to convey the land to this deponent's father, the said Malcolm Buchanan, upon paying only the expense of the purchase deed [and he] . . . soon thereafter settled upon the said tract, but which turned out to be 96 acres and . . . remained [there] until his death in or about the year 1833." Sworn on April 29, 1852.

"*Alexander Buchanan* of Portage within said County of Queens, farmer, maketh oath and saith that he is one of the sons of Malcolm Buchanan, deceased . . . [and] that the deponent is about 52 years of age, and hath always resided on his said fathers. . . farm. Deponent was sent to Charlottetown by his said late father expressly for the said deed of the said farm which was prepared by the late Charles Binns, deceased, from a survey of the said farm made by Henry Lobban, deceased, at which deponent was present. Deponent does not believe that his said father was present when his said deed was drawn or made out, otherwise deponent would have some recollection of his going to town for that purpose, as he could speak no English, and he must have taken some person to town with him for the purpose." Sworn on June 22, 1852.

"*John Cantelo* of Point Prim . . . farmer maketh oath and saith that . . . in the summer of the year 1818, deponent then being newly married at Pinette . . . was sent by his father-in-law to Charlottetown to see the late William Johnston, Esq., the Attorney and Agent for the late Earl of Selkirk at that time, and to obtain . . . the Pinette Mills. But deponent . . .was informed by him that he had already let the said Pinette Mills. Deponent then applied and asked for the Point Prim farm, but could not obtain it. And deponent then applied for . . . that tract of land laying between the Martins tract and the Portage clearance. . . between where O'Dogherty now possesses and the Martins tract. William Johnston then replied that he had nothing whatever to do with that land now, that it belonged to Nicholson, and stated further that there was plenty of land at Belle Creek or Wood Islands, but that there was no land handier. Wherefore deponent, who was a young man and was somewhat bashful, answered that he would see his father-in-law about it." Sworn on June 22, 1852.

"*Neil Morrison*, late a Merchant of Township 58, and now residing at Pinette in Queens County; maketh oath and saith, that he lived in the Dwelling House of the late Donald Nicholson of Portage, Belfast on Township 57 during the years from 1815 to 1822, as his principal confidential accountant and clerk and was intimately acquainted with all the said Donald Nicholson's business transactions, during the above period, having had charge of his cash and other books, up to the time, and subsequently to his leaving this Colony." Sworn on April 26, 1852.

[Published in *The Recaller*, September, October, and November 2000, "The Estate of John and Donald Nicolson of Portage".]

# The Affidavit of Margaret Munn

*Linda Jean Nicholson MacKenzie*

The majority of early Prince Edward Island probate files consist wills, inventories, bonds, and petitions – all standard legal documents offering varying degrees of information to the family historian or genealogist. But, occasionally a probate file will contain an affidavit which offers detailed information not found elsewhere.

One such document exists in the Estate File of Donald Shaw.[1] Donald Shaw had arrived on the Island in 1806 on the ship *Spencer*.[2] He settled in Strowan, Lot 34 and died there prior to April of 1814. It appears he may have died unexpectedly, as he did not leave a valid will. Probate law dictated that Donald's estate be divided between his next of kin. But, his estate was heavily in debt and Donald's sister Margaret, perhaps recognizing that there would be little or no assets left to divide, filed a claim against her brother's estate. To substantiate her claim, Margaret submitted an affidavit containing details of her immigration to Prince Edward Island:

"Margaret Munn, wife of Malcolm Munn of Wood Islands . . . maketh oath and saith that in the year 1806 this deponents brother, the late Donald Shaw of Strowan, Lot 34, came to this Island from Colonsay, Scotland, leaving this deponent, his only sister, to attend her aged mother, then sick in bed. That her said brother had been married a number of years before he left Scotland and had no children. And when going away, told this deponent to remain with her mother until the death of her mother (then soon expected) and that when he should hear of his mother's decease, he would send for deponent to this Island, and that deponent should be heir to all his property and afterwards wrote deponent to the same effect. And deponent further saith that her said brother wrote to her in the year 1810 and sent the letter by Mr. James Robertson, late of this Island, and therein stated to deponent that her passage was paid for and that she was to sail in the first ship for this Island, and repeated his former promises that deponent should have all his property, if she survived him and his wife. And deponent came to this Island, as requested, and went to live with her said brother and remained with him for upwards of three years and worked very hard indeed during all the said time, both indoors and out for her said brothers benefit. And deponent did not stipulate for any particular wages or salary, she having the future expectation held out to her as above mentioned. And deponent is of the opinion that she is well and justly entitled to wages at twelve shillings and six pence per month, at least, for three years payable out of the estate of her said late brother, making the sum of twenty-two pounds, ten shillings. And deponent . . . hath not received any payment . . . whatsoever for the said sum. And deponent, not knowing the value of those letters from her brother, hath long since allowed them to be destroyed or lost as useless or waste paper. And deponent, still hoping to keep the property he left, this deponent did not before furnish any claim or account to Mr. Peter Stewart, the Administrator of the said Donald Shaw.

her<br>Margaret X Munn<br>mark

Sworn at Chambers in Charlotte Town in said Island this 9th day of August 1820, being first Distinctly read to Deponent Before me Robert Gray"[3]

Administrator Peter Stewart noted in his final account that in 1821 he paid Malcolm Munn the wages due to his wife, and that had also paid Colonel Fraser, "an agent for the brothers of the deceased". After the estate was settled, a balance of 2 pounds and 15 shillings was left in the hands of the Administrator, who commented it was "too little to reimburse me for my time, trouble and expenses in this business".[4]

[1] "Administration of the Estate of Donald Shaw", Estate File No. Adm. S-24, Estates Division of the Supreme Court, Charlottetown.
[2] *The Island Magazine*, "PEI Passenger Lists: Part Three" (Fall/Winter 1977).
[3] "Administration of the Estate of Donald Shaw".
[4] *Ibid.*

[Published in *The Recaller,* May 2001.]

---

Speaking at the 150th Anniversary Celebrating the arrival of the Selkirk Settlers on August 6, 1953, well respected historian Malcolm MacQueen corrected the misconception that the name "Belfast" was a corruption of an earlier French place name. He explained, "Lot 57 was granted by the crown in 1767 to Samuel Smith and his brother, Capt. James Smith, of the Royal Navy. Their home was Belfast, Ireland, and in honor of it they called the district Belfast. Capt. Smith, then in command of the *Mermaid,* made two visits to this Island in 1770 of about six weeks duration."[1]

In his second book *Hebridean Pioneers,* published five years later, MacQueen would reveal his source – a letter, dated November 1770, and published in the March 1771 issue of the *Gentleman's Magazine* (London, England). The writer explained that Capt. Smith had visited Lot 58 which was, "called Prim by the French, but he [Capt. Smith] intends to name it Belfast, after a village in Ireland". MacQueen stated that the letter seems to remove any doubt that the Scottish settlement of Belfast was indeed named for Belfast, Ireland.

[1] *The Guardian*, August 7, 1953, p.7.

# Notes on Little Sands

*Annie MacMillan*

There is nothing more fascinating than the tales of long ago and it is too bad we are unable to obtain more information, but we will pass on a few items of interest along our historic shores of Little Sands.

The hardships our forefathers endured are beyond our imagination today. I think the most outstanding is the mail taken from Pictou, Nova Scotia in winter by Sandy MacMillan, better known as "Uncle Sandy". He was a native of Little Sands. He crossed on the ice and made this hazardous trip with a small boat, as the Straits would not be frozen over at all times. When he reached Nova Scotia he had to travel by a foot path through dense woods to Pictou, pick up the mail, and return the same way back to Prince Edward Island.

An interesting place to look in on in the early 1800's was "Beaton's Cove", now known as "MacPherson's Cove". Here was a busy little place where many ships were built, lumber was hewn and sawed from the nearby woods. A trench was dug and can still be seen. There was a School on this same location. Farther along the shore the first lobsters were packed in Duncan Munn's factory.

A Grist Mill was started around 1840 by Robert Dixon, Belfast. He ground wheat into flour and also made oatmeal. The large stones used are still to be seen on the site where "Grandma's Cabins" are now situated.

In 1905, a company started boring for coal along the shore on Dixon's. But, it was a pipe dream and they went from whence they came.

[Published in *The Recaller*, October 1984.]

**Gristmill stone.** In a gristmill, grains were ground into meal. Two stones similar to the one above were needed for a gristmill to operate. These stones often weighed a ton or more. One stone would stand stationary on the floor of the mill, while the second spun above, nearly touching. As the stones turned, their grooves crossed much like razor blades, cutting the grain. The miller adjusted to the distance between the stones to regulate how finely the grain was ground.

# Chapter Two

❧⚬❧

# Churches

"The church was the lodestone around which centered the life of the people.   Young and old alike presented themselves to divine service clothed in their best, and comported themselves in a manner befitting the sacred nature of the service."

- Malcolm MacQueen, *Skye Pioneers and "The Island"*.

**St. Andrew's United Church at Vernon Bridge.**  Opened and dedicated in March of 1969, St. Andrew's replaced six former churches: (top) Orwell Corner, Cherry Valley, Millview, (bottom) Pownal, Vernon River, and Orwell Head. [Photo courtesy of St. Andrew's United Church.]

# St. John's Presbyterian Church

*The Guardian*, August 3, 1953.

St. John's Presbyterian Church was erected in 1824. It is a beautiful structure forty-two feet wide and sixty feet long. The "wren" steeple is composed of a tower fourteen feet wide and sixteen feet long and surmounted by a steeple 85 feet high. There is a gallery running along both sides and one end. Perhaps the most remarkable thing about the construction of the building is the shingles which were all made by hand with an instrument called a "frow". It was a wedge-shaped blade with a short stout handle placed at right angles. The "frow" was driven through the block of wood with a wooden mallet and each shingle thus made was planed by hand. These original shingles, over 130 years old, secured with iron nails, made by the local blacksmith, still are in a remarkable state of preservation on the walls of the church.

Inside is a plaque to the memory of the first minister, Rev. John MacLennan, who was their spiritual leader from 1823 until 1849. Also commemorated are the memories of Rev. A. MacLean Sinclair and Rev. Allan Fraser, who was the first theological student from the district.

[Published in *The Recaller*, July 1994.]

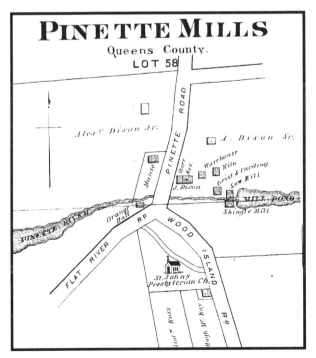

**Meecham's 1880 Atlas.**
In 1880, the Wood Islands Road was located behind St. John's Presbyterian Church, as shown on this map. During the 1950's, when the roads were being paved, the Wood Islands Road (now called the "Garfield Road") was moved to its present location in front of the church, cemetery and Polly monument.

*Prince Edward Island Register*, March 6, 1824, p. 3.

---

"Hector McKenzie of Flat River, Queens County, Farmer maketh oath and saith . . . that in or about the year one thousand eight hundred and twenty-five, the late Reverend John McLennan . . . resided at deponents house in Flat River aforesaid, being about the second year after [he] . . . came to this country from Scotland. And deponent saith that the late William Johnstone, Esq. Agent and Attorney for the Earl of Selkirk at that time, used at the said time to stop and reside at deponents house also when he visited the locality to see after the said early tenants. And that in the same year last aforesaid deponent was present with the said late William Johnston and the said late John McLellan at deponents said house, and this deponent expressed his dissatisfaction with the locality and position of a certain farm of land which the said Earl Selkirk had granted to the said John McLennan, and which deponent concerned to be in a bad neighborhood. And . . . the said Mr. Johnstone then replied and said that there was no other land in the neighborhood vacant that he could grant to the said late Mr. McLennan. ."

- Affidavit of Hector McKenzie, June 22, 1852, Chancery Court.

[Published in *The Recaller*, November 2000, "The Estate of John and Donald Nicolson of Portage, Part Three" by *L. J. N. MacKenzie*.]

# The Reverend John MacLennan

*Katharine MacLennan*

[Condensed from an address given by Katharine MacLennan, granddaughter of Rev. John MacLennan, at the 150th Anniversary of St. John's Church on August 5, 1974.]

The first minister of Belfast Church (1823 to 1849) was Rev. John MacLennan. He was born in 1797 in a small village in Ross Shire, Scotland; graduated with an M.A. degree from Kings College, Aberdeen in 1818; was licensed for the ministry of the Church of Scotland, November 22, 1822; and was ordained on April 23, 1823, to qualify him to accept the pastoral charge at Belfast, Prince Edward Island.

In September 1823, he and his young bride (nee Catherine McNab) reached Pictou, Nova Scotia. He was inducted into the charge of Belfast by the Rev. Donald Fraser and the Rev. Kenneth J. MacKenzie.

The district of Belfast, in 1823, included a large tract of land in the southeastern corner of P.E.I., from Point Prim to Cape Bear. The people also came to his ministry at Belfast from Seal River, Tea Hill, Portage, and Three Rivers (Georgetown). The population of the Selkirk colony had increased to nearly 4,000. Part of this was from emigration, but part from natural increase. From the Baptismal Records, we find Rev. MacLennan baptized 62 children in his own area in the first year, and 39 in the following year.

Soon after arriving, Rev. MacLennan started plans for the building of a new church. There was a log church, near the French Cemetery, which dated from the very earliest years of the Selkirk Settlement. This had served as both church and school. Now, as the settlement grew and extended into the back country, a more central location was required. Tenders for the building of a church 60 ft. long, 42 ft. wide, and 19 ft. post were invited March 6, 1824.

Rev. MacLennan returned to Scotland in the summer of 1849, returning to P.E.I. to fetch his wife and family of seven children. Two other children had died here, including a little girl three years of age who had drowned in the stream near Belfast Church.

In September of 1851, while visiting a child sick with diphtheria (in the Parish of Kilchrenen, Argylshire where he was serving), he contracted the disease and died within a few days. He was buried in the churchyard of Kilchrenen where his tombstone still stands.

The Rev. John MacLennan had served his Lord faithfully, and the influence of his ministry in Belfast has carried on to this day.

[Published in *The Recaller*, July 1994.]

---

# Early St. John's Church Records

The Baptismal records of Rev. John McLennan, the first minister of the Belfast District are a valuable tool for genealogists who are tracing their family roots. Rev. McLennan kept very good records, even recording the mother's maiden name and often adding other items of information and identification. The Baptismal Records are available at the Prince Edward Island Public Archives and Records Office in Charlottetown.

The first page of the Belfast Register of Baptisms is as follows:

*Baptized at Pinette 12th October, 1823.*

Duncan McMillan & Mary Shaw in Wood Islands, a daughter, born 24th Jany. 1823 Mary.

James Shaw & Henrietta McNiel, same place, a daughter, born 16th Decemr 1822 named Ann.

Magnus McDonald & Flora McMillan, Cape Bear, a daughter, born 15th March 1823 named Mary.

John Nicolson & Mary MacLeod, Orwell, a daughter, born 20th March 1823 _ named Marion.

5.     Samuel Martin & Margaret Martin, Orwell, a son, born 12th Novr. 1822, named Alexr.

6.     Donald MacDonald & Margt Nicolson Orwell Point, a son, born 15th May 1823, named Archd.

7.     Malcolm McLeod & Rachel McQueen, Gallows Point, a son, born 23rd Decr 1822, named John.

8.     Charles Nicolson & Mary McDond, Orwell, a daughter, born 10th April 1823 named Catherine.

9.     Charles Gillies & Isabella Nicolson, Orwell, a son born 20th June 1823, named Alexr.

*Baptized 18th October.*

10.    Donald McRae & Janet McRae, Wood Island Road, a son, born 12th May 1823 named Duncan.

11.    Alexr McKenzie & Eliza McDonald, Flat River, a son, born 18th Augt 1821, named John

12.    & a son, born 10th June 1823 named Alexr.

13.    Neil McEachern & Christina Stewart, Wood Island Road, a daughter, born 24th April 1823, Catherine.

*Baptized 22nd October.*

14.    Simon McKinnon & Janet McEachern New Town a daughter, born 14th Septmr 1823 named Jane.

---

*Baptized at Pinette Church 22$^{nd}$ Octr. 1823*

15.   Murdo McLeod, Taylor & Mary McLeod Orwell head, a son, born 12$^{th}$ June 1823 named Alexr.

16.   John McDonald & Flora McDougal, Pinette, a daughter, born 13$^{th}$ Decemr 1822 Mary.

17.   Charles McEachern & Margt McKinnon, Portree – a daughtr, born 16$^{th}$ Febr 1823 Marie.

The second page begins thus:

*Baptized at Pinette Church 22$^{nd}$ October 1823.*

15.   Alexander, son of Murdo McLeod, Tailor, and Mary McLeod, Orwell Head, born 12$^{th}$ June 1823.

*29$^{th}$ Octr*

18. Alexr. Stewart Taylor & Isabella Stewart, New Town Road, a daughtr born, 24$^{th}$ April 1823

   Janet.

19. William Rofs & Nancy Fair, Pinette, a daughter, born 25$^{th}$ May 1823 named Eliza.

20. Samuel Nicolson & Flora McLeod, Pinette road, a daughter, born 16$^{th}$ April 1823 Henrietta.

21. Colin McKenzie & Ann McKenzie, Wood Isd. Road, a son born 18$^{th}$ July 1823 Kenneth.

22. John McRae, a widower, Pinette Ponds, a daughter, born 17$^{th}$ Augt 1820 named Mary Ann.

The following is the last entry in the Baptismal Register by Mr. McLennan:

*September 18$^{th}$ 1849.*

Children of Angus Nicholson and Catherine McKinnon, Point: John, born 12$^{th}$ June 1845; Catherine, 10$^{th}$ May 1847; and (2884) Flora, 12 April 1849.

The following entries are at the end of the book, but not in Mr. McLennan's handwriting:

Baptized by the Rev. John McLennan at Charlottetown, 19$^{th}$ September 1849: Francis Longworth, son of John McNeill and Penelope McNutt, born 7$^{th}$ December 1848.

Baptized by the Rev. John McLennan at Charlottetown: (2886) John, son of Donald McDougall and Ann Gillies, born 15$^{th}$ October 1848.

Mr. McLennan left Belfast on September 19, 1849.

[Published in *The Recaller*, July 1994.]

# "Rest in Peace"

*Research by Joyce Kennedy.*

The beautiful, well maintained and tended cemetery of the historic St. John's Presbyterian is a point of pride in the church and the community. The cemetery, which now covers several acres, is well laid out and apparently well planned, with a grid of access roads forming a number of (roughly) square and equal sized sections.

The cemetery was not originally planned thus. These changes were made in the fall of 1894. And, as with all change, the construction of roads or "streets" in the cemetery was also met with objection.

The following letter was published in the March 21, 1895 edition of *The Patriot*. Mr. Neil MacDonald obviously felt that the dead of Belfast should not be disturbed to satisfy the whims of "some parties who are not long in the settlement."

> "SIR, - I have seen a letter in *The Examiner* stating that a petition was to be sent to the Legislature praying for power to remove graves and make streets through the burying ground at the Presbyterian Church, Belfast, by some parties who are not long in the settlement as compared to the descendants of the first settlers in Belfast, who cleared the forest and secured the church ground to lay their dead to rest in. A burying place should never be disturbed for any show or pride. The work performed already has not proved favorable to their objects; they want more power.
>
> NEIL MCDONALD.
>
> Belfast, February 19th, 1895."

*The Report of the Congregation of Belfast* for the years 1900-1903 provides an interesting account of the work that was carried out, including an inventory of graves which were to be moved and an accounting of the number of volunteer hours for men and horses devoted to the task.

> "The special work done in the Cemetery consisted in making roads through it, in laying it out in proper lots, and in removing remains to suitable places as one family after another gave their consent. It was begun September 17, 1894, and carried on until near the end of November. The first thing done was to make the roads needed so far as they could be made without interfering with graves. The next thing was to finish the roads by removing remains. There were seven coffins removed September 28, twenty October 25, seven November 5, nine November 12, seven November 13, and three November 17. There were a few

removals afterwards. One hundred and thirty-seven persons gave more or less assistance freely, in carrying on the work. Some gave between thirteen and fourteen hours of work, a large number between six and seven hours, and a few between three and four hours. The number of hours of free work given amounted in all to 99½ days of ten hours each. The time worked by horses came to eight days of ten hours each. The cash receipts were as follows:

### Treasurer's Account

Received for repairing fence . . . . . . . . . $ 37.05
Expended on Fence . . . . . . . . . . . . . . . . <u>37.18</u>
   Balance due . . . . . . . . . . . . . . . . . . . .13

### Mr. Sinclair's Account

Received for Improvements in Cemetery . $ 27.40
Received from Sale of Lots. . . . . . . . . . . . <u>20.50</u>
                               $ 47.90
Paid out for Work, & c. . . . . . . . . . . . . . . <u>47.00</u>

June 25, 1896 – Handed over to Treasurer. .  .90"

[Published in *The Recaller*, July 1994.]

**St. John's Presbyterian Church Cemetery before the 1894 restoration work.**
[Photo courtesy of Donald Garnhum. PAROPEI, 3466/Heritage Foundation 72.16.4.80.]

# Tea and Bazaar at Wood Islands Church

*The Patriot*, May 29, 1873.

The Presbyterian Congregation of Woodville [Wood Islands] and Little Sands intend having a Tea and Bazaar, D.V., early in July next, in the vicinity of Victoria Breakwater, the proceeds of which are to be applied in liquidating the debt on the new church at Woodville. Donations solicited from friends, for the above object, will be thankfully received by the following persons: -

| | |
|---|---|
| Mrs. D. McNeill, (Rev.) | Charlottetown |
| Mrs. D. Currie, | " |
| John McKenzie, Cabinet Maker, | " |
| Mrs. Donald McLeod, | Eldon, Belfast |
| Mrs. Capt. Rod'k McKenzie, | Flat River |
| Miss Sarah R. Morrison, | " |
| Mrs. D. Beaton, | in congregation |
| Mrs. Rod'k. Munn, | " |
| Mrs. D. Crawford, | " |
| Mrs. Duncan Munn, | " |

RODERICK MUNN,
Clerk of Congregation.

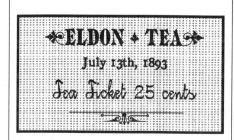

**Eldon Tea Ticket.**

At the turn of the century, teas were often held by community organizations and served as both fundraising and social events.

[Courtesy of Auldene MacKenzie.]

Wood Islands, May 24, 1873.

The above Tea and Bazaar will come off on Thursday, the 10th day of July, near the old Woodville Church. Tea on tables at 12 o'clock, noon. Tickets 24 cents each, to be had on the ground.

Should the day be wet, Tea will take place the following day.

RODK. MUNN.

[Published in *The Recaller*, June 1994.]

# Munificent Gift to Orwell Church

*The Guardian*, September 9, 1909.
Taken from Ross MacPherson's scrapbook.

Tuesday, the thirty-first day of August was a memorable day in the history of the Valleyfield Congregation. Precisely at ten o'clock, Dr. MacPhail of Orwell, Professor in McGill College, arrived at the new church now in the course of erection, with a magnificent bell which he presented to the congregation. The bell weighs nearly a ton and cost nearly one thousand dollars and was paid for by Dr. MacPhail together with the cost of erection and every incidental expense added thereto. Its tones can be heard for a distance of seven or eight miles. An address was presented to him on behalf of the congregation expressive of their thanks and gratitude for the splendid donation, to which the learned Doctor made a suitable and feeling reply.

On this magnificent bell is inscribed the following:

"Vivos voco, mortuos planco.
William MacPhail, 1802-1852
William MacPhail, 1830-1905
William MacPhail, 1859-1893."

**The bell donated by Sir Andrew MacPhail to the Valleyfield Church.**
[Photo courtesy of L. J. N. MacKenzie.]

Those inscriptions are appreciated when it is known that Dr. MacPhail's grandfather has his resting place in the cemetery at Valleyfield and no doubt for that and other reasons, the Doctor placed this monument of his respect in the Church tower. Long may it toll and long may the Doctor live to remind him of his generous gift.

[Published in *The Recaller*, September 1991. Editors Note: In June of 1971, the Valleyfield Church was moved to Montague and became the Hillcrest United Church. The bell donated by Dr. MacPhail is now displayed on the grounds of the MacPhail Homestead in Orwell.]

# Valleyfield Church

*The Guardian*, December 28, 1909.
Taken from Ross MacPherson's scrapbook.

John McPherson, the noted horse handler, has just finished moving the old Gospel Tent at Valleyfield to the new church lot. The unanimous thanks of the managers of the congregation was tendered him for the successful manner in which he performed such a difficult undertaking. This building was erected twenty-four years ago by D. L. McKinnon, Montague, and was used to accommodate the large crowds which gathered at communion and other services in the summer season. It is sixty-six feet square and the outside walls are eight feet high, and the centre is supported by two rows of heavy posts. It is now to be used as stables for horses during divine service.

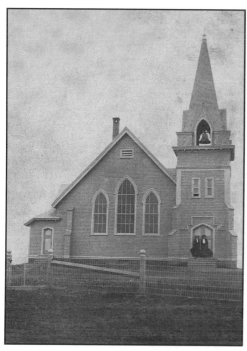

**This church was moved to Montague in 1971. A monument erected near the Valleyfield Cemetery commemorates the former location of this church.**

The finishing touches are being applied to the new church. The workmanship reflects great credit on the contractor, Jas. A. Martin. The pews are being installed by Mark Wright of Charlottetown and are of the most modern design. The pulpit, which is of quarter oak, is manufactured by the same firm, and is presented to the congregation by Mrs. Rev. R. McLean, to be in memory of her late husband, who was the much loved pastor of this congregation for over twenty years. The gift is much appreciated by the many warm friends of Mrs. McLean in this community. The new church is the design of C. B. Chappell, architect, Charlottetown, and is built under his supervision assisted by Hugh McPherson and John McLeod as inspectors. The opening services were held on December 26th, 1909. Morning service at 10:30, afternoon at 3 p.m. and evening at 7:30. The services of very popular clergymen were secured.

[Published in *The Recaller*, September 1991.]

# Rev. Donald MacDonald
## 1783-1867
*Hesta MacDonald*

Religion played a very central role in the life of early settlers on Prince Edward Island, and certainly in the life of the Belfast pioneers.

In the religious history of the still struggling colony of the 1800's, no footsteps resound more clearly than those of Reverend Donald MacDonald.

The history of the Church of Scotland in Prince Edward Island is closely woven around the life and ministry of that remarkable man. He was born in Perthshire, Scotland, and following his ordination in 1816, he labored as a missionary in the highlands until 1824. He then emigrated to Cape Breton, coming to Prince Edward Island in 1826.

His biographer writes: "He came to the Island and commenced his labors in the spirit of the true evangelist. To him, the toil of travelling over the country and ministering to the destitute was the highest pleasure. Multitudes flocked to hear him preach. In barns, dwelling houses, schoolhouses, and in the open air he proclaimed his commission to eager hundreds. Here and there he organized his bands of workers and ordained elders. He had no certain dwelling-place, no certain stipend, and bestowed all he got on works of charity . . . he was never married. . . his life work was over; and a great work it was. He had built fourteen churches; he had registered the baptism of two thousand two hundred children, and had baptized perhaps as many more not registered; he had married more people than any living clergyman; he had prayed beside thousands of deathbeds; he had a parish extending from Bedeque to Murray Harbour and from Rustico to Belle Creek."

The biography concludes, "The place of [his] interment was the Uigg-Murray Harbour Road churchyard . . . The funeral was the largest ever witnessed in the colony. All classes united in paying the last tribute of respect to the honored dead. The cortege numbered over three hundred and fifty sleighs. As the great procession moved down through the country, at the roadsides and at the doors and windows of the houses might be seen old men weeping; and women and children sobbing as if they had lost a father." The account ends by saying, "Reverend Donald MacDonald was laid to rest. A costly monument marks the spot."

[Published in *The Recaller*, Autumn 1982.]

# Chapter Three

❧❧❧

# Schools

"One of the hardest things to bear during the early years was the impossibility of getting adequate education.  Three or four generations passed before parents could afford higher education for their children."
- Malcolm MacQueen, speaking at the 150th Anniversary Celebrating the Arrival of the Selkirk Settlers, August 6, 1953.

**Hazel MacKenzie at the Ocean View School.**
[Photo courtesy of Tommy and Dora MacKenzie.]

# Four Schools

*Mrs. Marion (Roddie) MacKenzie*

By an interesting coincidence, the Belfast Consolidated Elementary School just completed in South Pinette is the fourth school built in this vicinity.

The first school in the Belfast area was built about 1807, at a distance of approximately 100 yards northwest of the present school. The second was built near the one recently vacated. The third was the one recently closed, and the fourth is the Belfast Consolidated Elementary School, now completed and open to pupils in the Belfast District.

In approximately 1807, the first school, a log cabin, was built in the Belfast area, a few years after the landing of the ship *Polly* in August 1803 with settlers from Scotland headed by Lord Selkirk. This was accomplished after these pioneers provided themselves with cabins, rudely constructed for their own shelter.

In Lord Selkirk's diary, he refers to two or three places in the "old French Village of Pinette", or where the French had settled many years before. Lord Selkirk speaks of these places as a few choice situations as regards to water, shore frontage, and many young birch trees that had grown up.

The first teacher in the log schoolhouse was Donald Nicholson. This first school was also used for religious meetings.

The log schoolhouse was burned, a second school was built about 1850, and the third school was built in 1906 by Malcolm MacKenzie – each becoming more modern, and climaxed by the "fourth".

Belfast Consolidated Elementary School, built on a spot overlooking Northumberland Strait, is the finest in modern architecture and furnishings.

Several of the present staff and students can proudly claim to be descendants of the "first teacher" and those noble pioneers who laid the foundation of education in our district.

[Published in *The Recaller*, November 1990 and April 2000.]

---

"During the first few years in the colony, facilities for formal education were of the most meager kind. Soon, however, well trained Skye schoolmasters opened up, in private homes, their little academies of learning, and here the neighboring children gathered for instruction."

– Malcolm MacQueen, *Skye Pioneers and "The Island"*.

# North Pinette School
# 1910

*From left, back row:* Merton Blake holding Russel Panton; *front row:* John Andrew MacDonald, John S. MacDonald, George Roy MacKenzie, David Blake, John Ross, Sinclair Ross, Baxter Ross, and Vere Penny.
*In background:* Gussie and Olive Buchanan. [Photo courtesy of Auldene MacKenzie.]

---

*The Canadian Teacher Magazine*, November 16, 1903:

Once upon a time Prof. Wilson, of Edinburgh, wrote on the blackboard in his laboratory:

"Prof. Wilson informs his students that he has this day
been appointed honorary physician to the Queen."

In the course of the morning he had occasion to leave the room and found on his return that a student had added to the announcement the words: "God Save the Queen."

- *Chicago Saturday Evening Herald.*

[Published in *The Recaller*, October 1986.]

# 1929 School Report

*Journal of the Prince Edward Island Legislative Assembly.*

Following is a list of schools and outstanding improvements:

**Bellevue** — New closet built. New blackboard provided.

**Belle River** — Partition removed, giving more room space. Windows to left and rear. Playground ploughed and harrowed. New furnacette placed in school.

**Caledonia** — Property remains unchanged.

**Culloden** — No improvements.

**Eldon** — New sills laid under building. School equipped with furnacette.

**Flat River** — School property in good condition.

**Grandview** — Furnacette placed in school.

**Heatherdale** — Sign-board placed. Roof shingled. Walls calcimined and wood-work painted.

**High Bank** — New book-case purchased.

**Hopefield** — Woodhouse supplied.

**Iris** — New woodhouse built.

**Little Sands** — New woodhouse under construction.

**Mt. Buchanan** — School property in good condition.

**Melville** — Interior of building calcimined. New outbuildings provided and general appearance improved.

**Newtown Cross** — New signboard placed.

**Newtown Lower** — Unsatisfactory lighting. Pupils face a window.

**Ocean View** — Property remains unchanged.

**Orwell** — No improvements. New floor needed.

**Orwell Cove** — Excellent new seats provided. Graded.

**Pinette South** — Property remains unchanged.

**Pinette North** — Improvements made to seats, teacher's desk, etc.

**Pt. Prim** — School building needs attention. Splendid new teacher's desk supplied by Capt. Murchison.

**Valley** — No improvements.

**Uigg** — Property somewhat neglected.

**Valleyfield West** — Property unchanged.

**Valleyfield East** — Property unchanged.

**Wood Islands East & West** — No change.

**White Sands** — Windows painted.

In conclusion allow me to express my appreciation for the help received from you and your staff in the work in which I am now engaged and for the kindness and hospitality extended to me by the good folk of the different districts through which I travel. I have the honour to be Sir,

Your obedient servant,

WM. A. MacPHEE

[Published in *The Recaller*, October 1994.]

**Ocean View, ca. 1938.** *From left, back row:* Margaret MacFadyen, Margaret MacKenzie, Marion MacKenzie, Esther MacFadyen, Doris Ross; *second row:* Danny MacLean, Roddie MacFadyen, and Florence MacKenzie; *front row:* Jimmy MacLean, Johnny MacLean, Tommy MacKenzie, Alexander MacKenzie, and Helen MacKenzie. [Photo courtesy of Johnny and Marie MacLean.]

# Belfast School Photographs

**Iona West, ca. 1928.** *From left back row:* Annie Roche, Mary McKenna; *second row:* Joan Byrne, Theresa McKenna; *third row:* Mary O'Shea, Margaret O'Brien, and Clara McGuigan. [Photo courtesy of Margaret Edmonds.]

**Mount Buchanan, June 1940.** *From left, back row:* John C. MacKinnon, Harold Larsen, Alfreda Cantelo, Bert Docherty, Florence MacLeod, Mary Nicholson, Grace MacDougall (teacher), Willard Nicholson, Lloyd Buchanan; *front row:* Florence MacKinnon, Gordon Morrison, Peggy Nicholson, Louis Larsen, Eliza Morrison, Freddie Martin, Sandy MacKinnon, Edna Nicholson, and Angus Nicholson. [Photo courtesy of Eliza Gillis.]

**North Pinette, ca. 1945.** *From left, back row:* Anne Docherty, Steven Compton, Annie Ross, Helen MacKenzie, Peggy Gillis, Mary Ross, Evelyn Ross, Joreen Docherty; *second row:* Frances Gillis, Boynton Panton, Earl Ross, Tommy MacKenzie, Helen West (teacher); *third row:* Charlie MacKenzie, Billy Ross, Neil Panton, Johnny Panton, Verna Ross, and Peggy Ross; *front row:* Bruce Singleton, Clayton Singleton, Gloria MacLeod, Vaunda MacTavish, and Grace Docherty. [Photo courtesy of Tommy and Dora MacKenzie.]

**Flat River School Closing, 1947.** *From left, back row:* Mary Ross (teacher), Gordon MacPherson, Sandy MacRae, Christine MacPherson, Kathleen Ross, Charlotte Ross (holding baby) Allison Ross, Jemima MacDonald, Florence Ross, Viola MacDonald, Nettie MacLeod, Sarah Ross, Katie Ann MacDonald, Minnie MacRae, Ollie Ross (holding baby) Elaine Ross; *second row:* Wilfred MacDonald, Gordon MacDonald, Elliott Wight, Martin MacRae, Scott MacPherson, Connie Ross, Helen Wight, Fanny MacPherson, Christine Wight, Bernice Knox, Etta Beaton; *third row:* Alvin MacDonald, Keith Nicholson, Frances Ross, Sterling Wight, Eleanor Ross, James Knox, Margaret Ross, Carol MacPherson, Lona Ross, Frances MacDonald, Jean Ross, Miriam MacPherson, Shirley MacDonald, Phyllis Ross, Alice MacPherson, Margaret MacKenzie, and Sandra MacKenzie. [Photo courtesy of Viola Gillis.]

*The Past is Before Us*

**Iona East, ca. 1949.** *From left, back row:* Lorna McCabe, Rose McKenna, Margaret Poole, Phyllis McCabe, Mary Mooney, Kevin McKenna, Eugene Mooney; *third row:* Florence McCabe, Jane McCabe, Joan McKenna, Bernadette McCabe, Alice McKenna, Irwin Connolly, Johnny McCabe; *second row:* Colleen McCabe, Joyce Connolly, Dunstan McKenna, Glenn McCabe, Marie McCabe, Marie Connolly, Gerard Mooney; *front row:* Merlin McKenna, Vincent Connolly, Rose Mooney, Joseph Mooney, Elaine McCabe, Shirley McGuigan, Shirley Connolly, Charlie McCabe, Lois Hughes, and Janet McKenna. Teacher Jack Hughes. [Photo courtesy of Florence O'Shea.]

**Point Prim, 1952.** *From left, back row:* Angus Murchison, Martin MacRae, Caryl MacRae, Alma Saunders, Rolla Murchison, Eliza Morrison (teacher); *second row:* Audrey Saunders, Joan MacLeod, Ann Murchison, Barbara Saunders, Donna MacRae; *front row:* Ernie Gillis, Stewart MacRae, Louise Saunders, Florence MacLeod, Judy MacRae, Anna Gillis, and Alberta Murchison. [Photo courtesy of Eliza Gillis.]

**South Pinette, April 1953.** *From left, back row:* Viola MacDonald (teacher), Diane Ross, Jeanette Cantelo, Jean Hubley, Beryl MacMillan, Angus MacMillan, Robert Ross, and Roland Hubley; *middle row:* Elizabeth MacKenzie, Donald Smith, Barbara Cantelo, Beverly Hubley, Betty Jean Hubley, Helen Hubley, Ida MacMillan; *front row:* Sterling Hubley, Donna Morrison, and Malcolm MacMillan. [Photo courtesy of Viola Gillis.]

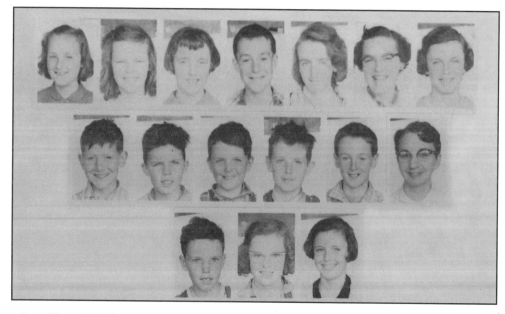

**Iona West, 1958/59.** *From left, back row:* Lavina Roche, Elaine McGarry, Marguerite Daley, James Edmonds, Mary Edmonds, Ursula Roche, Auralie Flynn; *second row:* Blair McKenna, Mickey Byrne, Brian Flynn, Michael Flynn, Emmanuel Edmonds, Verna Martell (teacher); *front row:* Kevin Daly, Geraldine Daly, and Pauline Flynn. [Photo courtesy of Margaret Edmonds.]

# Year End at Eldon School

*The Patriot*, July 24, 1933.

On Friday afternoon, June 30th, the annual examination of Eldon School was held. The increasing interest of the district in the school was well shown by the number of parents and visitors present.

The pupils were examined in the different subjects by their teacher Mr. Reginald MacLean, and by their ready answers showed that they had been well taught during the past year.

After the pupils were examined in the different subjects, the teacher then gave a short account of the work carried on during the past year.

The following prizes, donated by the teacher, were presented to those making the highest and second highest average in their grade for the year:

**GRADE IX**
1. Jean Halliday
2. Mary MacWilliams

**GRADE VIII**
1. N. S. Larrabee
2. Cassie MacPherson

**GRADE VII**
1. Alice Halliday
2. Marion MacMillan

**GRADE V**
1. James Halliday
2. Hampton Penny

**GRADE III**
1. Joyce MacDonald
2. Jean VanIderstine

**GRADE II**
1. David Gillis
2. Newton Penny
3. John MacPherson
4. Donald MacPherson
5. Vernon Finlayson
6. Irene Finlayson

**GRADE I**
1. Alvin MacPherson

Public School certificates were presented to N. S. (Buddie) Larrabee and Cassie MacPherson.

Very encouraging remarks were made by a number of parents on the quality of the work done, and how well the school is advancing under the careful guidance of the teacher who is engaged for the third term.

After singing the National Anthem, the pupils were treated to ice cream and cake by the members of the Women's Institute.

[Published in *The Recaller*, September 1993.]

# Christmas in the One Room School

*Mary Ross*

Christmas concerts in the one room school on Prince Edward Island were more than a program of Christmas songs, drills, and dialogues. The concert was the coming together of all families in the district. It was a giving of Christian love and friendship, a time when parents got to meet other children.

As the teachers prepared suitable parts for each grade or pupil and got on with rehearsing, the mothers at home were sewing or purchasing new outfits for the children to wear at the concert.

The night of the concert arrived! There were no velvet curtains, no fancy back drops, and certainly no microphones. So, for the "wee" ones, it might be visual with the auditory missing, but their stage appearance was a delight. For the older pupils, it was a time to display their individual talents and have fun doing it.

**Point Prim School Concert, ca. 1950's.** *Left to right:* Santa (Manson Murchison), Dale Murchison, Neil Murchison, Jennie Murchison, Margaret Murchison, and Thelma Murchison. [Photo courtesy of Eliza Gillis.]

The arrival of a "native" Santa presented a guessing game and lots of merriment. The children waited for their name to be called. This gave each child another moment in the limelight. As the sound of Santa's sleigh bells could still be heard in the distance, all stood at attention for the singing of "God Save the King". Another highlight of the year ended and families wended their way homeward to put another log on the fire and have a much needed sleep.

[Published in *The Recaller*, November 1993.]

# The Country School

*Kenneth MacDonald*

In Prince Edward Island rural life and education had a special relationship. Because there was no local level of government at the rural and small village level, the school district filled the vacuum. The school formed the center of the community and the boundaries of the school district were synonymous with the perimeters of the community. When programs and plans were implemented, they were done within the confines of the school district. Although school districts legislated, other functions that took place within the school district were not.

The New Free Education Act of 1852 provided compulsory free education. The provision of buildings was enforced, but attendance of children was not. This act brought about a flurry of activity to establish school districts, erect schools, and procure teachers. Before this there were few schools. For example, in 1852 there were 133 schools on the Island.

In 1876 there were seventy-four districts without schools. By 1886 there were ten, but in eight of those ten districts new schools were being erected and provisions had been made for the remaining two – one through amalgamation and the other dismemberment.

Although schools were established expeditiously following the passage of the New Education Act, this did not mean universal free education through grade twelve level as it exists today. In fact, the first public high school was not opened until 1932. High schools were established in Montague in 1936 and Kinkora in 1941, with grade eleven taught in both schools. Both were in large settlements and were not consolidated schools.

By 1942 though, some schools were beginning to amalgamate. Older children, finding their own means of transportation, went from two or three districts to a centralized school. These schools were basically what today we would call junior high school. No basic change occurred to the school district as a result of this trend.

[Published in *The Recaller*, September 1996.]

# *Chapter Four*

ക്⊶◌

# *Businesses*

"The native honesty of the people [of Belfast] manifested itself in their business relations. To ask for security was unheard of. Promissory Notes were not in use, and refusal to honor an obligation was looked upon with great scorn."

- Malcolm MacQueen, *Skye Pioneers and "The Island"*.

**Compton's Sawmill, Belle River.** Built around 1897, this windmill drove a 32 inch rip-saw and some small machines. In 1915, the mill was torn down and a new building was erected. [Photo and information courtesy of Howard Hancock.]

# Belfast Mills

*Hesta MacDonald*

Today's mills deal principally with the sawing and milling of lumber, but equally important a few decades ago was the milling of wheat. Dixon's Mill, owned and operated by Milburn Dixon's father, provided stone-ground flour for his customers in Little Sands. One of the mill stones can be seen at the Netherstone Inn in Little Sands.

MacMillan's Mill in Wood Islands was equipped with rollers, and when the farmers took their wheat to that mill they could get four products: white flour, cream of wheat, shorts, and bran.

Across the road from MacMillan's Mill was a carding mill owned by George Young. Several other sawmills served the Belfast area, some are still operating, while others have long gone:

- Compton's Mill, Belle River.
- Danny John G's (Munn's) Mill, near Wood Islands Church.
- Lloyd MacMillan and George Stewart's Mill, Hopefield.
- MacEachern's Mill, near Hopefield Station.
- Cook's Mill, Wood Islands.
- Hancock's Mill, Belle River.
- Joe Dixon's Mill, Eldon (later Dan MacPherson's).
- Hughie MacPherson's Mill, Flat River.
- Ross's Mill, Roseberry.

[Published in *The Recaller*, November 1995.]

**MacPherson's Mill, Flat River.** First built by Alexander MacPherson and his sons, this sawmill was run by water power. Alexander died in 1929 and his sons continued to run the mill. It remained in operation until the early 1970's. [Photo and information courtesy of Miriam Bell.]

# D. E. Ross and Sons

*Mary Ross*

Mills were a focal point in the neighborhood. Grist mills were important because a major part of the Island's diet was made up of the grain byproducts. Sawmills provided the lumber for the shipyards in Orwell and Pinette. Woolen mills were also important as most farmers raised sheep. After shearing, the raw wool was taken to a carding mill.

The earliest record of a mill in this area dates back to the French period. This mill was at French Creek, on or near the site of the mill in Roseberry that was operated by Donald Ross until 1972.

Ross & Sons made a specialty of turning out what were called "shooks", thin lath-like material for the manufacturing of packing boxes of all shapes and sizes. The shooks were sold to exporters in Charlottetown, Summerside, and Souris.

The boards were planed, matched, grooved, and cut to the exact size, width, and length of the box desired. A special machine, reportedly costing the pricey sum of $800. at the time, pressed and wired the bundles of sides, ends, bottoms, and covers. The consignee or exporter would finish and assemble the boxes.

Garfield Ross, Donald Hughie's son, was the business manager of the operation during its heyday. He ensured that orders were filed and delivered, bills were paid and accounts receivable were collected. Garfield remembers that more than thirteen hundred dollars worth of berry boxes alone was shipped in the fall of 1927. This was due in large part to the great demand and production of blueberries. Later, boxes for shipping poultry and smelts joined Ross's inventory of manufactured products.

Unfortunately, the boom of the late 1920's couldn't last forever. We all know too well the devastation of the North American economy which followed the stock market crash of 1929. Thriving rural businesses like the mill in Roseberry, and others, felt the sting of the depression as well. But, perhaps most damaging to the business foundation of D. E. Ross and Sons was the widespread use of cardboard as a material for cartons and boxes. The wooden boxes were soon a thing of the past, and a big part of the business declined.

The mill stayed in operation until 1972 under the direction of Donald Ross. Adam Wight, who had come there to work as a young man, was one of the last sawyers to work at Ross's Mill.

[Published in *The Recaller*, November 1995.]

# Hopefield Sawmills

*Catherine Fraser*

The earliest sawing for building purposes in Hopefield was done by Robert Dixon, father of Milburn and Samuel Dixon, on his wood property near the County Line on the south side of Gray's Road. Here a framework or platform was built out from a high bank or hill to allow for rolling the logs onto it. Under the platform was room for a sawyer to stand with two or three feet clearance between his head and the bottom side of the log he was sawing. First the log to be sawed was flattened on opposite sides with a broad axe or by cutting wide slabs from it with the saw. Then corresponding lines were marked on both sides with a chalk line to guide the sawing. One flat side was then turned down and the sawing began. The two-man saw was wide at one end like a handsaw, and about six feet long. The teeth were designed to cut against the grain of the wood and to do most of the sawing on the down stroke. The sawyer on top had to lift the saw on the upstroke and guide it on the line when cutting. Not only must the man in the pit pull the saw when it was cutting, he had to keep watch on the cutting line with the risk of getting sawdust into his eyes.

An alternative used by some early sawyers was a framework or platform built at ground level with a spacious and deep pit dug underneath for the sawyer to work in. Although the men in those primitive sawmills changed positions periodically, it took a lot of back breaking work, and long hours when wages were less than one dollar per day to produce enough lumber to build a house or barn.

The next stage in sawmill development came in 1908 when Benjamin MacEachern, assisted by his son Cyrus, built a steam sawmill. This mill that employed workers from surrounding areas was situated near the railroad on the west side of the County Line. The site was a scene of activity during the winter months as men hauled sleigh loads of lumber that they had piled there to be processed in the spring. Sawing began in March. From the well insulated engine room came the chug and hissing sounds of escaping steam, and there are memories of the deep shrill blast of the mill whistle as it sounded to call the men to work, signaled the lunch hour, and announced the end of the day's work.

In 1919 a fire destroyed the sawmill, but in the following year it was replaced and a grocery store added. Misfortune struck again when the second sawmill was leveled by fire. Cyrus MacEachern and Harry Bonnell then became partners and a new mill was opened in 1921. Cyrus, after a time, went to British Columbia to work there as an accountant to a lumber company. The Hopefield sawmill under the management of Harry

Bonnell continued to serve the community until 1933 when the business was again interrupted by another fire.

The next sawmill, also powered by steam, was built in 1937 by Lloyd MacMillan and George Stewart, Wood Islands. They purchased the site from Alexander MacGregor on Gray's Road, west of the County Line. When MacMillan and Stewart enlisted in the service of World War II, the property was purchased by Thomas Gosbee and Sons, Murray Harbour, who eventually replaced the steam engine with the more efficient diesel. Gosbee and Sons operated the sawmill between lobster fishing seasons until 1984.

There were two smaller mills in the district in the 1940's. One was built and operated for a short time by Daniel Harris MacLeod at his property on the County Line Road, and another by World War II veteran Raymond Munn, on the north side of Gray's Road, a short distance east of Hopefield School. This sawing operation was in progress until Raymond left the district for England in 1948.

Lumber to be processed has now to be hauled to sawmills in Wood Islands, Murray River and other outlying communities.

[From *Hopefield and its Families, 1856-1989*, by Catherine Fraser. Published in *The Recaller*, November 1995. Reprinted with permission of the author.]

---

## Pinette Mills to be Let.

*With immediate possession,*
*for one or three years,*
*As may be agreed on.*

These Mills are situated on Township 57, formerly held by Mr. Edward Poole. The Grist Mill and Kiln are nearly new, and the Saw Mill is in good order. They are centrally situated for business, and well worthy the attention of a person of some capital and industrious habits. None need apply but persons of good character and who can give satisfactory security (if required) for the payment of rent.

The above property is part of the Estates of the *Earl of Selkirk*, and well worth the attention of practical Agriculturists. A most favourable opportunity presents itself to Farmers of small capital, desirous of purchasing tracts of Wilderness Land from 50 to 100 acres each, as many miles of new roads are now making through his Lordship's different Estates in Prince Edward Island, which consequently affords a very rare opportunity for selecting good sites for farms.

Emigrant Farmers arriving in this Colony, with capital, will be afforded every information, *free of any expense*, by applying to the Subscriber, who can offer them some other very valuable and highly improved Landed properties.

All applications by Letter must be post paid.

May 26th, 1843.                    W. DOUSE.

[*The Islander*, 9 June 1843.]

---

# Ross's Store

*Hesta MacDonald*

*" 'Twas a great store for buying and selling. You would
take over a basket of eggs and would get a big order of
groceries. They were so friendly . . . we missed them."*
— Catherine MacDonald

One hundred years ago, in 1895, Mr. A. D. Ross opened a general
mercantile business in rented premises at the mouth of the Wharf Road in
Eldon, just across the road from where Cooper's Store now stands. When
the store burned in 1912, Mr. Ross bought the store owned by Wellington
Mutch. Although it was located on the corner now occupied by Cooper's,
at that time its main door was facing the Wharf Road. Mr. Ross later
turned the store around to face the main road.

The other store in the village during the early part of the century was
Shad and Moore, opposite the store later operated by Martin MacDonald.
Mr. Ross was a staunch Conservative, and when that political party was in
power, the Court House was located above Ross's Store. But, political
patronage was such that when the Liberals won an election, the court
would move to Mr. Moore's premises.

Lena Martin MacEachern recalled that Ross's Store
was referred to as "the most up-to-date country store of
that time". It served as a center of the community where
local residents bartered for groceries and men gathered
to exchange stories.

Years brought changes. As cars became prevalent, the long shed for
the horses was no longer needed, and pumps were installed for selling
White Rose gasoline. Sons Dave and John, and daughter Eleanor
succeeded their father in the business. David served in the army during
World War II, and was a prisoner of war, but returned to the retail
business after the war ended.

Early in the 1950's, as the Trans Canada Highway was being
constructed from Wood Islands to Borden, the roads had to be widened.
Ross's Store was one of the buildings that had to be razed, to be replaced
by the present day store.

Following David's death in 1960, the store was sold, but the
community retains pleasant memories of the sixty-five years when Ross's
Store provided a fine service in the Belfast area.

[See also "We Remember Lena Martin MacEachern" which immediately follows.
Published in *The Recaller*, June 1995.]

---

# We Remember Lena Martin MacEachern
## 1902-2001
*Mary Ross*

Lena Martin MacEachern was born in Newtown in 1902 to John and Catherine (MacLeod) Martin. There she attended the one-room country school where she did well, but at age 14 she realized that money for college would be a problem, and like many young ones at that time, she decided to take a job.

In 1916, at age 15, Lena went to work at A. D. Ross's store in Eldon. Lena's description of the store and her work there is fascinating. The Ross Store seemed to be the hub of the community. It was a three story modern structure with an elevator used to transport goods to the basement.

The first floor of the store was the busiest, as it housed groceries. There were bins installed along the counters to hold bulk goods such as sugar, beans, tea, soda, and cream of tartar. These had to be weighed and packaged according to the specifications of each customer. The second floor of the store contained dry goods, wallpaper, paint, dishes, pots and pans, shoes and some clothing.

**The *Harland* heading toward Halliday's Wharf.**
[Photo courtesy of Elinor Gillis.]

Merchandise for the store came on the *Harland*, a boat that docked at Hallidays Wharf in the summer. Tom MacLennan with his team of horses would then haul the goods to the store. In the winter, they were picked up at the Iona train station. The store exchanged oats and eggs with local farmers for other groceries and purchased fresh cut meat from Patty Corish, a butcher from Keppoch.

Lena worked at the Ross Store with Etta MacWilliams (bookkeeper), six days a week, from 8 am to 10 pm. Their only holidays were Christmas and New Years.

Lena was paid $7.50 a month and ate two meals a day with the Ross's. She praised the Ross family and described them as very clever business people. Lena enjoyed catering to the customers. Most customers were nice, but some expressed dissatisfaction with prices. Still, Lena would not undersell prices set by her boss. Two other stores, James St. Croix Moore's and Jim Larrabee's, were nearby if a customer wanted to try and get a better deal.

When the local men gathered in the evening and sat on nail kegs or at the counter, their conversations entertained Lena as she worked. She overheard the news of the district – who was sick, who had a baby, who got married, and even who had a fight. The "Nail Keg Meetings" were an important part of her day. After cleaning up and securing the doors, Lena would walk home.

In 1923, Lena left her job and married Monty MacEachern, and went to live in their home in Garfield. She continued her work with the church, the Women's Missionary Society, Women's Institute, and Sunday School. She also took an active part in concerts at the Belfast Hall (built in 1924). The Eldon Orchestra, comprised of Eddie Martin (Lena's brother), James Halliday, and Herb Worth, were always on hand to supply music.

In 1925, the MacEachern's moved to Newtown where they continued to be a focal part of the district. Many singsongs and house parties took place at their home. At Sunday evening hymn sings, Lena would play the pump organ to accompany the singers. Their two sons, Charlie and Gordon were part of their life now, so Lena became involved in the Young People's Groups with the church where she supplied the music and helped with Bible Study.

In later years, Lena and Monty moved back to the old MacEachern Homestead in Garfield. Work was not as important, and she and Monty took trips to Western Canada to visit their son Gordon.

In 1974, Lena lost her soul mate of 51 years. She accepted this as part of life and she continued on and enjoyed her family and friends.

**Lena Martin MacEachern.**
[Photo courtesy of Mary MacEachern.]

Mother's expect that their children will outlive them, but this was not for Lena, as she lost a daughter-in-law and later her two sons. Instead of viewing life as grim, she counted her blessings – her grandchildren and her daughter-in-law Mary MacEachern.

Lena faced advancing years with calmness and fortitude. The last chapter of Lena Martin MacEachern's life closed on March 7, 2001 when she died at Eldon in her 99th year.

[Published in *The Recaller,* April 2001.]

# MacDonald's Store

*Mary Ross*

Years ago, the pulse beat of the community was the General Country Store. Martie MacDonald's store in Eldon was typical, as related by his widow, Estelle: "Martie and I ran the store together from 1936 to 1957. The store was old, old, when we came here, and afterwards the Post Office and the telephone (exchange) were in that building.

We lived in Lyndale before that. Martie was a World War I veteran of the 105th Regiment. He was awarded the Military Medal for bravery in the field.

A lot of goods were sold in bulk – weighed out and tied up with a string. Some bulk items were beans, tea, sugar, coffee – crackers were sold in bulk too. Matches were 10 cents for a big box. Royal yeast cakes were another items used in every household. Each item was listed in the counter book, priced, then added up in your head.

The variety of goods was endless. Besides food, we sold buckets, shovels, hay forks, stove pipe, coal scuttles, horse rugs, yard goods, thread, thimbles, paint, nails, horseshoes, pen nibs, ink, Sweet Caporal cigarettes, and plugs of Twist chewing tobacco.

We sold flour by the barrel. Feed for livestock too – we had a warehouse full of that.

Children came to buy penny candy or a 5 cent chocolate bar, all displayed in delicious array in a glass showcase. Years later, after we got electricity, they came for a 5 cent ice cream.

What a relief to get electricity in the store! I still see those old kerosene lamps hanging up, and the dimly flickering light to work by. We didn't have a telephone at first, either.

Oh yes, there would be a barrel of herring, and dried cod fish in boxes. There were puncheons of oil, of molasses, of vinegar. I can see it yet, the carcass of a cow hanging from a nail – someone would bring it in to pay a bill, you know.

What I enjoyed best about keeping store was the contact with people. Men came in the evenings to talk and to buy food and other goods – shoes, overalls, fleece-lined underwear, woolen yarn, or patent medicines, cough medicines, or Epsom salts. Poor old Dave (Dr. David MacKenzie, Sr.), many an evening he spent sitting on the counter and talking with the men. There was a neighborly atmosphere.

We had gas tanks too, but there were few cars in 1936, and the roads were in poor shape for the few cars there were.

Of course, our store wasn't the only one in the village. Ross's Store was in operation; Jim Larrabee had the store there for awhile. When they put the road through (Trans Canada Highway) that store was torn down and the new one was built farther down the road (now Cooper's Grocery).

We worked hard, both Martie and I. We opened the store at 8 am, six days a week, and we stayed open evenings also. But, it was a family enterprise, and I missed it terribly after we closed out the business."

[Published in *The Recaller*, October 1991.]

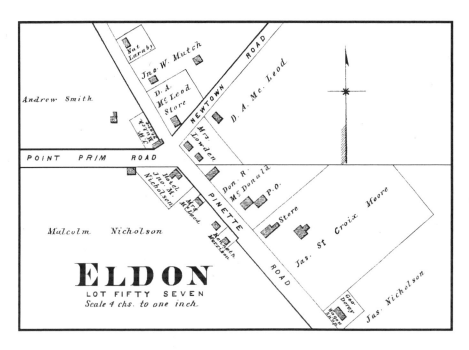

**Meecham's 1880 Atlas showing the village of Eldon, Belfast District.**

In the early 1900's, every community had a local store. Father Arthur O'Shea described Iona's local store in his community history *It Happened in Iona*, "when we speak of 'the store' we refer in particular to the one operated until recently by Leo and Florence O'Shea at Iona Corner which had its beginning in or about 1875 with John O'Connell as its first merchant."

# The Butter Factory

*Hesta MacDonald*
*With Research by Ernest MacLeod*

The eighty-nine year history of the Federal Dairying Company (The Butter Factory) came to a close on March 31, 1990, the closing date for the butter factory at Eldon.

When the company had started in 1901, it borrowed $1800 to get the necessary building and equipment to begin operations. The first secretary, S. A. Nicholson, got the handsome sum of $75 a year for his work, while the butter maker was paid $48 a month. In the first two or three years of operation, the butter maker had a helper who was paid by the company, but thereafter he had to provide for his own helper.

**The Federal Dairying Company (Butter Factory) in 1910.**
[Photo courtesy of Eliza Gillis.]

The minute books indicate that John D. MacRae was hired from 1901-1915, initially as a helper, but for many years the butter maker. From 1917-1936, Rupert Hubley occupied the position. Faber Dreelan followed for one year. Then, from 1938 until 1972, the butter maker was Aage Larsen, with family members, in turn, serving as his assistant.

Initially, farmers sent their milk to the factory where the cream was separated from the milk and tested for butterfat. Haulers picked up the milk and delivered it to the factory. From the outset, the quality, purity, and taste of the butter were of prime concern. Early minutes record, for example, that milk from cows feeding on marshes would not be accepted because the marsh hay affected the taste of the butter. By-laws specified even the height of the milkstands to be used by the patrons. Butter was sold to the wholesalers in Charlottetown, and probably in Halifax.

The first factory was located across the road from Sam Frizzell's store. When the Trans Canada Highway was being built, a new plant was constructed. This major decision is given one sentence in the minutes of the annual meetings of 1953 and 1954, and the 1955 minutes read: "After a lengthy discussion on the new plant, the meeting was adjourned."

Two business items of perennial concern to the directors were the procuring of ice and the disposal of buttermilk. Each patron was required to haul three (later four) loads of ice to the factory each winter, or pay fifty cents per load in lieu of ice. Part of the building was used for ice storage. Finally, in 1952, the ice question was left in the hands of the directors.

Another important item was obtaining fuel. In the early years, the company bought wood, but later it changed over to coal.

By the 1980's, it became increasingly difficult to get cream for butter production, as farmers began raising more beef cattle, replacing their dairy herds. Another change was the selling of milk rather than cream, as more and more farmers abandoned their "separators" in favour of bulk tanks on their farms. In 1982, the company began to explore the possibility of changing their product to a blend of butter and margarine, but that did not take place because of the high cost of equipment required.

James Halliday, the last president of the Federal Dairying Company, conducted the 1990 annual meeting at which the decision was made to close the factory. Montague Dairy purchased the equipment, supplies, and fuel. The butter inventory was sold separately. The land and building were also put up for sale.

An important page of the economic history of the Belfast area had come to an end, having served well its time and generation.

[Published in *The Recaller*, September 1995. Editors Note: The records of the Federal Dairying Company may be found at the Prince Edward Island Public Archives and Records Office in Charlottetown, Accession 4710.]

---

Taken from Bobs West's scrapbook. Submitted by Helen MacDonald:

"Much credit is due to Mr. Moore for the interest he has shown in agriculture by his experiment with the silo. A year ago it was an article of faith with most farmers that ensilage could not be a success on Prince Edward Island. But, thanks to the progressive spirit of Messrs. Moore, Miller, and Dr. Morrison of St. Dunstan's and others, the success of the silo in P. E. Island has come to be an established fact. With the ensilage of 1¾ acres and a trifling amount of meal, Mr. Moore has kept two cows in excellent condition since the first of November."
- Belfast Jottings, May 1894.

# We Remember Aage Larsen 1907-1977 and Algunda Larsen 1905-1988

*Hesta MacDonald*
*With information from Margaret Larsen Panton, Harold and Aletha Larsen, Lester and Gloria Larsen, and Louis Larsen.*

It must have been a heart-wrenching experience for the young Larsen couple when Aage embarked alone for Canada. The year was 1928, and Canada must have seemed very far away from their home on the Island of Laeso in Denmark.

Aage and Algunda were married on October 30th, 1927, and it was after the birth of their first child, Tobie, that she came to join her husband on P.E.I. It was a difficult voyage for a young mother, and Algunda later attributed the rigorous ocean crossing as contributing to the death of the infant Tobie. The baby died shortly after arrival on the Island, and was laid to rest in the North Tryon Presbyterian Church cemetery.

Aage had found employment in a butter factory in Tryon, where he learned the skills of butter making. He advanced rapidly, and when a butter maker was required by the Federal Dairying Company for its plant in Eldon, Aage Larsen was awarded the job. . . a job he held from 1938 until his retirement in 1972.

**Aage and Algunda Larsen at their 40th Wedding Anniversary in 1967.**
[Photo courtesy of Margaret Panton.]

When the Larsens moved from Tryon to Belfast, they first lived in a house in Newtown (later owned by Earl Gay), but they soon moved to Mount Buchanan where they established a successful farming operation.

Ten children were born to the Larsen couple between the years 1929 and 1945. Algunda had a happy disposition, "always singing" as she went about her work. They made certain their children had a Christian upbringing in St. John's Presbyterian Church, where Aage served as an Elder for many years.

It was a strong family unit, with the children learning the skills of farming and homemaking as they worked with their parents. Several family members worked in the butter factory. Son Harold remembers wrapping the two pound blocks of butter in the special butter paper.

Later, a one pound butter printer with a design on the top came into use. (Harold went on to work for ten years in a large butter making operation in Ontario, where he no doubt used some of the skills he learned at his father's knee.) Daughters Florence and Bessie later worked with their father in the butter factory as well.

Thrifty and industrious, Aage and Algunda soon made the farming operation a prosperous living. In 1958, the crops did exceptionally well, and the couple made their long dreamed about trip back to Denmark to visit family and long-ago friends.

Aage and Algunda were happily planning their golden wedding anniversary for October 30, 1977, but that was not to be celebrated. Aage passed away early in that month. Algunda survived him until September 8, 1988. In addition to their sons and daughters, there are now many descendants. Their 38th grandchild was expected at the time of Aage's death, and when Algunda died eleven years later, they had 105 descendants. All this from two people who bravely left their homeland to make a life in a new land.

It was a good day for Belfast (and for all of P.E.I.), when the Larsens moved into the district. They were fine citizens and good neighbors, and Belfast was fortunate in having them decide to make their home here. Indeed, we fondly remember them.

[Published in *The Recaller*, September 1995.]

# Chapter Five

❧❧❧

# Community Service

"There was a feeling of co-operation [in Belfast] which did much to make life not only tolerable, but actually enjoyable."
- Malcolm MacQueen, *Hebridean Pioneers.*

**Rev. S. D. MacPhee. Minister at St. John's Presbyterian Church from 1906 to 1909.** [Photo courtesy of L. J. N. MacKenzie.]

# New Channel at Wood Islands

*The Islander*, September 16, 1859.
Contributed by Mrs. Margaret Smith.

About 7 o'clock a.m., the inhabitants of Wood Islands, Belle Creek, Little Sands, and Rona[1] began to assemble until upwards of one hundred persons were present, each with a shovel, and began digging as eagerly as if they were obtaining the precious metal in the gold regions of California or Australia; and the beach near the intended canal was a scene of gratification to behold the banners flying on both sides, and to hear the melodious pipes of Mr. McLauchlan who headed a great number of workmen to the spot. Among the other banners which rendered the place so peculiarly picturesque, I observed the Conservation Poll Flag of Belle Creek with the following inscription:

"Clannaibh na'n Gaeil ri guailibh a Cheita" –
"The Highlanders shoulder to shoulder",

testifying to the unity that still exists among the inhabitants of this section of Queens County.

As the men were digging, superintended by Mr. Donald McMillan, it was not neglected by Mr. John Douse, of Charlottetown, who took an active part in the matter, and other members of the Committee of Management, to provide some refreshment for them, as they had previously intimated to the Committee that that day would be gratis, notwithstanding the urgent demand of the harvest.

Many of the ladies kindly left their domestic affairs to prepare the necessary repast, and at one o'clock the workmen were invited to dine upon the Little Islands, when it was ascertained that 103 persons were present.

About 2 o'clock they again repaired to the Canal, resumed their labour, and continued working until sunset, when all returned to their respective homes, highly pleased with the labour of the day.

The original channel is nearly closed, and in all probability the water will have its course through the new passage about the 30th instant. Suffice it to say, the whole work is progressing beyond our most sanguine expectations.

By Order of the Committee,
D. Crawford, Sec'y.
Wood Islands, September 9, 1859.

[Published in *The Recaller*, June 1981.]

[1] Mount Vernon.

# We Remember Allan Finlayson
## 1898 - 1991
*Hesta MacDonald*

Sixty-seven years ago Allan Finlayson came to Eldon to ply his trade as a blacksmith. He worked in his shop (where his son Vernon later had his garage) until he retired in 1976 at the age of 78.

**Allan Finlayson.**
[Photo courtesy of Brenda MacDonald.]

Smithing had been a family trade for generations. His grand-uncle, whose forge was in Pinette, was the first blacksmith in Selkirk's colony.

Blacksmithing was an extremely important trade before the days of cars. Allan made farm implements and parts for farm machines, and also parts for stoves and household equipment. Putting rims on wagon wheels and wheels for machinery was another part of his work. He prided himself on his ability to shoe horses, even the crossest or most nervous one. Only one horse ever left his shop without shoes and when it was taken to Proude and Moreside in Charlottetown, they said, "If Allan Finlayson can't shoe it, we won't even attempt it without the stocks."

Once, in the 1950's, a horse stopped the bus that ran from Wood Islands to Charlottetown. It was a wild horse and very frightened. Allan had one hind hoof in his lap and started to hammer the first nail when the horse bolted, taking its owner with it. When the horse was finally halted in the middle of the road, Allan was still holding the hoof. He finished nailing the shoe on the road, then the bus driver, who had obligingly waited, gave a cheerful wave and drove off.

Allan Finlayson died in 1991. He was predeceased by his wife and their son Vernon. His daughter Irene lives in Nova Scotia. Allan will be recalled as a good neighbor and a fine blacksmith.

[Published in *The Recaller*, September 1993.]

# Belfast Postmasters

*Linda Jean Nicholson MacKenzie*

When Prince Edward Island entered into confederation on July 1, 1873, the 179 Island post offices came under federal jurisdiction. Of these, 12 post offices were located in the Belfast area (Lots 57, 58, 60 and 62).

By 1910, the total number of Island post offices had increased to 460. But, when rural delivery and mail carriers were introduced in 1912-13, a majority of small rural post offices were closed. By 1921, there were only 125 post offices on the Island. This number was further reduced when consolidations were made in 1968 and 1969.[1]

Following is a list of Belfast post offices compiled from the National Archives of Canada database which were active from 1874 to the present day.

[1] Murray, G. Douglas. *The Post Office on Prince Edward Island (1787-1990)*, 1990.

**BEATON'S MILLS**, Lot 60. Est. pre 1 Apr. 1875. Closed 15 Apr. 1966.

| Postmaster | Appointed | Vacated | Cause of Vacancy | Notes |
|---|---|---|---|---|
| D. Beaton | 1 Apr. 1875 | 27 Feb. 1893 | Resigned. | |
| Roderick McLeod | 1 Dec. 1893 | 23 Feb. 1903 | Death. | |
| Miss Christina McLeod | 1 July 1903 | 23 Nov. 1910 | Resigned. | |
| John S. McLeod | 27 Dec. 1910 | 1 Sept. 1914 | Change of Site | |
| Campbell McLeod | 26 Oct. 1914 | 1924 | * | |
| W. J. Emery | 20 May 1924 | 28 Oct. 1929 | Resigned. | |
| Peter John Emery | 28 Mar. 1930 | 1 Apr. 1964 | * | Born Apr. 1892 |

**BELFAST**, Lot 57. Est. pre 1 July 1874.

| Postmaster | Appointed | Vacated | Cause of Vacancy | Notes |
|---|---|---|---|---|
| James Moore | 1874 | 4 June 1881 | Resigned. | Appt. pre1874 |
| Martin Martin | 1 Jan. 1882 | 1896 | Change in Site | |
| Mrs. Jessie McDonald | 1 Nov. 1896 | 1918 | Death. | |
| Isabella McDonald | 15 Aug. 1918 | 31 May 1944 | Resigned. | Born May 1864 |
| Eleanor Charlotte Ross | 1 June 1944 | Acting | | |
| Mrs. Catherine Elizabeth McDonald | 29 July 1944 | 1 Mar. 1958 | Resigned. | |

| Postmaster | Appointed | Vacated | Cause of Vacancy | Notes |
|---|---|---|---|---|
| Mrs. Esther W. Gillis | 1 Oct. 1958 | Acting | | |
| Mrs. Esther W. Gillis | 17 Dec. 1958 | 29 Apr. 1970 | * | |
| Mrs. A. C. MacColl | 30 Apr. 1970 | | * | |
| Connie MacInnis | 1 June 1983 | Present | | |

## BELLE CREEK, Lot 62. Est. pre 1 July 1874. Name changed to "Belle River" on 21 Feb. 1967.

| Postmaster | Appointed | Vacated | Cause of Vacancy | Notes |
|---|---|---|---|---|
| James Cook | 1874 | 10 July 1883 | Resigned. | Appt. pre1874 |
| Charles Cook | 1 Jan. 1883 | 1885 | Resigned. | |
| Lemuel Compton | 1 July 1885 | 21 Dec. 1886 | Resigned. | |
| Daniel McLaren | 1 Apr. 1887 | 12 Jan. 1917 | Death. | |
| Alexander W. McLaren | 9 July 1917 | 7 Sept. 1923 | Resigned. | |
| John Blue | 15 Oct. 1923 | 28 Sept. 1931 | Resigned. | |
| Duncan J. Riley | 29 Apr. 1932 | 7 Nov. 1945 | Resigned. | Born 20 Aug. 1878 |
| John Ewen Cook | 27 Nov. 1945 | 29 Aug. 1950 | Resigned. | |
| Alexander A. Beaton | 18 Nov. 1950 | Acting | | |
| Alexander A. Beaton | 11 Jan. 1951 | 11 Aug. 1951 | Resigned. | |
| Alexander R. Compton | 6 Nov. 1951 | 24 Aug. 1953 | * | |
| Miss Priscilla Bell | 19 Aug. 1953 | Acting | | Born 19 Aug. 1900 |
| Miss Priscilla Bell | 16 Oct. 1953 | 31 Mar. 1968 | Replaced. | Born 19 Aug. 1900 |
| Mrs. Annie Mae Bell | 1 Apr. 1968 | | | |

## CALEDONIA, Lot 60. Est. pre 1 July 1874. Closed 31 Oct. 1929.

| Postmaster | Appointed | Vacated | Cause of Vacancy | Notes |
|---|---|---|---|---|
| James Walker | 1874 | 1879 | Change of site | Appt. pre1874 |
| Malcolm M. Stewart | 1 July 1879 | 25 July 1887 | Resigned. | |
| John McDonald | 1 Jan. 1888 | 13 Nov. 1897 | * | |
| Angus J. McLeod | 1 Dec. 1897 | 21 Nov. 1898 | Resigned. | |
| Mrs. Mary Stewart | 1 May 1899 | 1929 | Death. | |

## FLAT RIVER, Lot 60. Est. pre 1 July 1874. Closed 31 Aug. 1915.

| Postmaster | Appointed | Vacated | Cause of Vacancy | Notes |
|---|---|---|---|---|
| R. K. McKenzie | 1874 | 29 June 1906 | Resigned. | Appt. pre1874 |
| Alex. Balderston | 1 Oct. 1906 | 6 Jan. 1912 | Resigned. | |
| Malcolm R. Beaton | 1 Mar. 1912 | 18 Feb. 1915 | Resigned. | |

## GARFIELD, Lot 58. Est. 1 Aug. 1882. Closed 3 Apr. 1915.

| Postmaster | Appointed | Vacated | Cause of Vacancy | Notes |
|---|---|---|---|---|
| George McKenzie | 1 Aug. 1882 | 9 June 1902 | Death. | |
| Thomas McKenzie | 1 Sept. 1902 | 22 Jan. 1911 | Resigned. | |
| John A. McKenzie | 1 May 1911 | 6 June 1912 | Change of site. | |
| Angus W. McLeod | 29 June 1912 | 3 Apr. 1915 | Closed. | |

## IRIS, Lot 62. Est. 1 Oct. 1885. Closed 31 Dec. 1918.

| Postmaster | Appointed | Vacated | Cause of Vacancy | Notes |
|---|---|---|---|---|
| Angus Beaton | 1 Oct. 1885 | 1912 | Death. | |
| Angus A. Beaton | 31 Oct. 1912 | 26 Feb. 1913 | Resigned. | |
| Roderick A. McBeth | 31 Mar. 1913 | 31 Dec. 1918 | Closed. | |

**LEWES**, Lot 60. Est. 1 June 1908. Closed 30 June 1918.

| Postmaster | Appointed | Vacated | Cause of Vacancy | Notes |
|---|---|---|---|---|
| Ewen McKinnon | 1 June 1908 | 8 Mar. 1913 | Dismissed. | Pol. Partisanship |
| George McLean | 31 Mar. 1913 | 30 June 1918 | Closed. | |

**MONTAGUE CROSS**, Lot 57. Est. pre 1 July 1874. Name changed to "Iona" 1 Apr. 1903. Closed 30 Nov. 1967.

| Postmaster | Appointed | Vacated | Cause of Vacancy | Notes |
|---|---|---|---|---|
| William Callaghan | 1874 | 6 Dec. 1876 | Left the place. | Appt. pre1874 |
| Patrick A. Callaghan | 13 Mar. 1877 | 23 May 1892 | Resigned. | |
| John O'Connell | 1 Sept. 1892 | 16 June 1893 | Resigned. | |
| Joseph McCabe | 1 Sept. 1893 | 6 Sept. 1905 | Dismissed. | Pol. Partisanship. Born May 1859 |
| Bernard Martin | 10 Oct. 1905 | 26 Apr. 1912 | * | |
| Joseph McCabe | 6 June 1912 | 14 Aug. 1942 | Death. | Born May 1859 |
| Miss Mary McCabe | 20 Aug. 1942 | Acting | | Born 30 Sept. 1898 |
| Miss Mary McCabe | 15 Sept. 1942 | 17 May 1961 | Death. | Born 30 Sept. 1898 |
| Mrs. Annie Florence Rooney | 18 May 1961 | Acting | | Born 5 Dec. 1895 |
| John Sterling Creamer | 13 Sept. 1961 | 23 June 1964 | Resigned. | |
| Mrs. Florence O'Shea | 3 July 1964 | Acting | | |
| Mrs. Florence O'Shea | 5 July 1965 | 30 Nov. 1967 | Closed. | |

**MOUNT BUCHANAN**, Lot 57. Est. 1 Dec. 1889. Closed 16 July 1913.

| Postmaster | Appointed | Vacated | Cause of Vacancy | Notes |
|---|---|---|---|---|
| Donald Stewart | 1 Dec. 1889 | Sept. 1901 | Death. | |
| Margaret P. Stewart | 1 Feb. 1901 | 12 Aug. 1902 | Resigned. | |
| John G. McRae | 1 May 1903 | 1906 | * | |
| Calvin Bishop | 1 Feb. 1906 | 22 Jan. 1913 | Dismissed. | Pol. Partisanship |
| Mrs. Sarah Smith | 15 Feb. 1913 | 16 July 1913 | Closed. | |

**NEWTOWN CROSS**, Lot 57. Est. 1 Aug. 1884. Closed 13 Aug. 1965.

| Postmaster | Appointed | Vacated | Cause of Vacancy | Notes |
|---|---|---|---|---|
| James Cody | 1 Aug. 1884 | 28 May 1912 | Change in site. | |
| William Cody | 3 June 1912 | 30 Apr. 1933 | Death. | |
| Miss Georgina Cody | 4 July 1933 | 18 Sept. 1933 | Resigned. | |
| Michael Morrisey, Jr. | 31 Oct. 1933 | 13 Aug. 1965 | Closed. | Born 2 Mar. 1896 |

**OCEAN VIEW**, Lot 58. Est. 1 Dec. 1906. Closed 13 Aug. 1965.

| Postmaster | Appointed | Vacated | Cause of Vacancy | Notes |
|---|---|---|---|---|
| John Bruce | 1 Dec. 1906 | 22 May 1912 | * | |
| Malcolm McLean | 1 June 1912 | 4 Apr. 1922 | Resigned. | |
| John T. Weatherbie | 22 Dec. 1922 | 4 Feb. 1931 | Death. | |
| Angus Martin McLeod | 29 Apr. 1931 | 15 Feb. 1960 | * | Born 17 Mar. 1888 |
| Mrs. Mary Kathryn MacKenzie | 29 Apr. 1960 | 13 Aug. 1965 | Closed. | |

**ORWELL COVE**, Lot 57. Est. pre 1 July 1874. Closed 27 Aug. 1954.

| Postmaster | Appointed | Vacated | Cause of Vacancy | Notes |
|---|---|---|---|---|
| E. Morrisey | 1874 | | | Appt. pre1874 |
| Andrew Stephens | | 1878 | Death. | |

*The Past is Before Us*

| Postmaster | Appointed | Vacated | Cause of Vacancy | Notes |
|---|---|---|---|---|
| Mrs. Mary Stephens | 1 July 1878 | 28 Nov. 1896 | Resigned. | |
| Charles Nicholson | 20 Jan. 1897 | 3 Nov. 1899 | Resigned. | |
| Donald D. McLeod | 1 May 1900 | 5 Apr. 1939 | Death. | |
| Ernest McLeod | 11 Apr. 1939 | Acting | | |
| Ernest McLeod | 3 Aug. 1939 | 7 May 1954 | Resigned. | |

## PINETTE, Lot 58. Est. 1 Aug. 1877. Closed 30 June 1918.

| Postmaster | Appointed | Vacated | Cause of Vacancy | Notes |
|---|---|---|---|---|
| Donald McDonald | 1 Aug. 1877 | 6 Nov. 1880 | Resigned. | |
| Angus Young | 1 Apr. 1881 | | Cancelled. | |
| Mrs. Margaret Campbell | 1 June 1881 | 8 Sept. 1882 | Resigned. | |
| R. Stevenson | 1 Apr. 1883 | 12 Mar. 1888 | Resigned. | |
| Malcolm McLeod | 1 Oct. 1888 | 26 Sept. 1891 | Resigned. | |
| Theo. Lantz | 1 Feb. 1892 | 30 Mar. 1893 | Resigned. | |
| Alexander F. McDonald | 1 Jan. 1894 | 11 Oct. 1917 | Resigned. | |
| | | 30 June 1918 | Closed. | |

## POINT PRIM, Lot 58. Est. pre 1 July 1874. Closed 31 July 1913.

| Postmaster | Appointed | Vacated | Cause of Vacancy | Notes |
|---|---|---|---|---|
| M. N. Murchison | 1874 | 1874 | Change of site. | Appt. pre1874 |
| John McDonald | 1 Apr. 1875 | 30 Sept. 1883 | Resigned. | |
| Archibald McRae | 1 Jan. 1884 | 1894 | Change of site. | |
| Angus Murchison | 2 July 1894 | 31 July 1913 | Closed. | |

## RONA, Lot 60/62. Est. pre 1 July 1874. Name changed to "Mount Vernon" on 1 July 1899. Closed 31 May 1918.

| Postmaster | Appointed | Vacated | Cause of Vacancy | Notes |
|---|---|---|---|---|
| N. McKenzie | | 1874 | Resigned. | Appt. pre1874 |
| William McQueen | 1 Aug. 1874 | 1879 | * | |
| Norman McKenzie | 1 July 1879 | 5 Oct. 1895 | Resigned. | |
| J. L. Morrison | 1 Feb. 1896 | 29 Dec. 1903 | Death. | |
| Mrs. E. Townsend | 1 Mar. 1904 | 1909 | * | |
| W. J. Davey | 25 Feb. 1909 | 12 Feb. 1914 | Resigned. | |
| William Boughner | 23 Mar. 1914 | 31 May 1918 | Closed. | |

## ROSEBERRY, Lot 58. Est. 1 Nov. 1895. Closed 31 Mar. 1915.

| Postmaster | Appointed | Vacated | Cause of Vacancy | Notes |
|---|---|---|---|---|
| Murdoch Morrison | 1 Nov. 1895 | 1907 | Death. | |
| | | 31 Mar. 1915 | Closed. | |

## SELKIRK ROAD, Lot 60. Est. pre 1 July 1874. Closed 31 Mar. 1918.

| Postmaster | Appointed | Vacated | Cause of Vacancy | Notes |
|---|---|---|---|---|
| John Dougherty | 1874 | 1875 | Removal of PO | Appt. pre1874 |
| Alex. A. McKenzie | 1 May 1875 | 15 June 1883 | Resigned. | |
| James Callaghan | 1 July 1883 | 3 Nov. 1891 | Death. | |
| Francis Dougherty | 1 July 1892 | 30 July 1900 | Resigned. | |
| Maurice Shea | 1 Mar. 1901 | 25 Mar. 1912 | Change in site. | |
| Patrick Kelly | 15 May 1912 | 31 Mar. 1918 | Closed. | |

## WOOD ISLANDS, Lot 62. Est. pre 1 July 1874. Closed 16 Oct. 1915.

| Postmaster | Appointed | Vacated | Cause of Vacancy | Notes |
|---|---|---|---|---|
| John Kennedy | 1874 | 15 Mar. 1881 | Resigned. | Appt. pre1874 |
| George Offer | 1 June 1881 | 28 Dec. 1891 | Resigned. | |
| Hector M. P. McMillan | 1 Mar. 1892 | 21 Feb. 1895 | Death. | |
| Mrs. Mary McMillan | 1 Apr. 1895 | 31 Oct. 1906 | Resigned. | |
| Mrs. Mary McPhee | 1 Dec. 1906 | 27 July 1907 | Resigned. | |
| Neil Peter McMillan | 1 Sept. 1907 | 16 Oct. 1915 | Closed. | |

## WOOD ISLANDS, Lot 62. Est. 1 Apr. 1889. Name changed from "Wood Islands North" 21 Feb. 1967. Closed 17 Oct. 1969.

| Postmaster | Appointed | Vacated | Cause of Vacancy | Notes |
|---|---|---|---|---|
| D. Crawford | 1 Apr. 1889 | 22 Feb. 1897 | * | |
| John H. McMillan | 1 Apr. 1897 | 27 Apr. 1901 | Death. | |
| Mrs. Flora McMillan | 1 July 1901 | 27 July 1906 | Resigned. | |
| John G. McLeod | 8 Oct. 1906 | 18 Nov. 1915 | Change of site. | |
| William M. Crawford | 1 Dec. 1915 | 7 Apr. 1928 | Resigned. | |
| Donald M. McLeod | 7 May 1928 | 12 Oct. 1932 | Dismissed. | Pol. Partisanship. |
| John A. McKenzie | 1 Nov. 1932 | 11 Jan. 1936 | Dismissed. | Pol. Partisanship. Born 6 Sept. 1888. |
| Donald M. McLeod | 25 Feb. 1936 | 10 Feb. 1947 | Death. | Born 28 Feb. 1874. |
| Mrs. Katie J. MacLeod | 14 Feb. 1947 | Acting | | Born 23 June 1892. |
| Mrs. Katie J. MacLeod | 29 Mar. 1947 | 1 July 1964 | * | Born 23 June 1892. |
| Mrs. Alvina Jane Emery | 24 Nov. 1964 | 17 Oct. 1969 | Closed. | |

## WOOD ISLANDS WEST, Lot 62. Est. 1 Nov. 1905. Closed 15 Mar. 1932.

| Postmaster | Appointed | Vacated | Cause of Vacancy | Notes |
|---|---|---|---|---|
| James A. McMillan | 1 Nov. 1905 | 2 May 1910 | Death. | |
| Allan J. McMillan | 1 June 1910 | 15 Mar. 1932 | Closed. | |

* In compliance with the Privacy Act (1983), some personal information was deleted from this file.

[Published in *The Recaller*, November 2001.]

---

*Mae Gilmore Buchanan:*

I remember that 1926 was referred to as "the winter of the big snow". At that time our only communication for passenger, mail or freight services was the train. Of course, road ploughs were unheard of, and the small train plough had little effect on the huge drifts that piled up, day after day, in the deep railroad cuttings between the Fodhla (Iona) and Melville stations. Local men, my father among them, relayed the snow up those deep cuttings using only hand shovels – happy to earn some extra money in their effort to "get the mail through".

[Published in *The Recaller*, October 1994.]

# We Remember Dougald MacKinnon
## 1886-1970
*Mary Ross*
*With information from Blair MacKinnon*

Dougald MacKinnon was born at Mount Buchanan on December 15, 1886, the son of John MacKinnon and Flora Caroline MacLeod. He was educated at the local school, but his education did not end there. He was a great reader, with a particular interest in local history and the history of the American Civil War. He had an uncle who had fought in that conflict, and it was a highlight of Dougald's life when he traveled to the United States and toured many of the Civil War battle sites. An interest in his Scottish heritage came naturally to Dougald as well. He was a direct descendant of Flora MacDonald, made famous as the girl who hid Bonnie Prince Charley from the English after the Battle of Culloden. Another ancestor, Dr. Angus MacAulay, had been a leader of the Selkirk Settlers and had served as Speaker of the House in the Provincial Assembly.

Dougald was first elected to the Legislature in the general election of

**Dougald MacKinnon.** [Photo Courtesy of Willena MacKinnon.]

1935, after years of being active within his party and his community. He was re-elected in 1939, 1943, 1947, 1951, and 1955. He announced his retirement from active politics in June 1959, after a distinguished career as a parliamentarian and a member of the Executive Council. He served as Minister of Public Works and Highways, and later as Minister of Industry and Natural Resources.

In his community, Dougald was very active in bettering the economic life of the district. He had been one of the principal people involved in establishing the Fisherman's Union, which improved prices for local lobster fishermen. He was also largely responsible for the successful establishment of the Northumberland Ferry Co., Ltd. in Wood Islands, providing a vital transportation link with the mainland for farmers and others to move their produce from southern Kings and Queens counties.

Dougald was married to the former Mary Sarah MacWilliams of Eldon. They had two children, Marion and John.

[Published in *The Recaller*, April 1996.]

---

# Country Doctor

*Hesta MacDonald*

A few excerpts from the memoirs of Dr. Stewart MacDonald, who served the Belfast district from 1953 to 1959 illustrate how much conditions change in a few brief years:

When Dr. Stewart MacDonald went to Eldon, paved roads were very few and the Trans Canada Highway from Eldon to Charlottetown had not been constructed. Eldon village boasted electricity, but the far corners of the community were still without it. All the communities east of Eldon and all the back roads had no thought of electric lights.

When Dr. MacDonald left Eldon in 1959, both paved roads and electric wiring were realities over much of the area. Both those commodities made life a great deal easier and more comfortable for the rural doctors, but the biggest change and the one which revolutionized country practice came shortly after the P.E.I. government instituted Medicare across the province.

Twenty-five years ago, most people lived out their lives in their homes and most times, when people died, the doctor was there attending the death and comforting the families.

**Dr. Stewart MacDonald.** [Photo courtesy of Hesta MacDonald.]

Dr. MacDonald was no stranger to Eldon, nor unaware of the rigors of a country practice. He was born in Little Sands during a savage March blizzard and he often heard the tale of the difficulties Dr. Brehaut from Murray River had faced to be present at his birth.

Generations of Dr. MacDonald's ancestors lie sleeping in the Belfast church cemetery and he claims relationship with many people in Belfast, his mother having been a Stewart from Belle River.

Many the story Dr. MacDonald can tell of hard travel he endured during snowstorms and on muddy March and April roads. Once his jeep got stuck in a mud hole so deep that it took three tractors to haul him out.

Road conditions dictated the method of travel. For several months of the year, he drove a jeep, although later he also acquired a Volkswagen. When roads were at their worst, he traveled by sleigh, wood sled, tractor, or snow plough. He often used snowshoes to respond to emergency calls. He slogged through the mud on foot. The heavy medical bag he carried was stocked with pills, potions, and penicillin.

"Most people in the country appreciated having a doctor within call", Dr. MacDonald says. Many people helped him in various ways. An invaluable helper was a bachelor named Herbie Worth. In Herbie's lifetime, he traveled thousands of miles over all kinds of roads, helping each doctor that came to Eldon. [See also "We Remember Herbie Worth" which follows this article.]

Despite the hardships, country practice provided some very happy memories for Dr. MacDonald. He says he remembers every baby he brought into the world, "including a few sets of twins".

One time, Dame Flora MacLeod, clan chieftain, was on a visit from Scotland and she visited the Prince Edward Island Hospital. "It just happened I had three new born MacLeod babies in the nursery that day and so I was introduced to Dame Flora. She was very gracious and pleasant. We chatted a few minutes before she left me with an injunction to take good care of all those new MacLeod's", Dr. MacDonald says.

[Published in *The Recaller*, Autumn 1982.]

---

# We Remember Herbie Worth
## 1910-1970
*Hesta MacDonald*

*"He gained from Heav'n*
*('twas all he wished) a friend."*

- Gray's Elegy

Many long-time residents of Belfast and generations of school children in the area cherish warm memories of Herbie Worth, who died September 19, 1970.

Herbie is remembered for neighborliness, musical talent, and kindness to children. When I asked one man what I should say about Herbie, the answer came without hesitation, "Say he was always good to kids."

Born in Charlottetown in 1910, Herbie came to Eldon after the death of his parents, Frank and Mary Worth. Then 13 years of age, he moved into the home of Lauchie and Mary Ross, who always treated him as a son, and he responded with filial devotion as long as they lived.

Although of a pleasant, happy disposition, there was a trace of sadness whenever he spoke of his parents and his little brothers from whom he was parted while a child. His younger brothers were adopted and given new surnames – Eddy Morrison, Lawrence Rowe, and Jack MacDougall (Jack later resumed the surname Worth). Gordon, Victor, and sister Bertha (Mrs. Hudson Hardy) were the other siblings.

**Herbie Worth, 1963.** [Photo courtesy of Edna MacLeod.]

Herbie farmed for a living, but it soon became evident that music was his real interest. He was always glad to share his musical talents – playing the fiddle for dances, singing at church, participating in local entertainment, and assisting teachers with music for school concerts. He is fondly remembered by both teachers and pupils who testify that there was never "a generation gap" with Herbie.

Each local doctor in turn discovered Herbie to be an invaluable helper, who was always willing to accompany him when he had to make house calls during storms or blizzards, or when roads were at their muddy or snowy worst.

An interesting conversationalist and story teller, he was a welcome guest among people from all walks of life. Mothers knew that their children never learned anything but good, in speech or deed, from him, and children sensed that his interest in them was genuine. One best describes Herbie as "gentlemanly" in the truest sense of the word.

Herbie had no descendants, but there is seldom a gathering of people in Belfast at which his name is not spoken, some story about him retold, some kind deed of his recounted.

Truly, it may be said of him, "To live in the hearts of our friends is not to die."

[Published in *The Recaller*, May 1994.]

# The Community of Belfast

*The Guardian*, August 15, 1894.

## ORWELL HEAD.

The land is more distinctly marked here by hill and dale, consequently the mind flits away to Scott's "Land of brown heath and shaggy wood. Land of the mountain and the flood." Here the Presbyterians have a beautifully located church, and to the eastward, across the valley which smiles between stands the church where the late Rev. Donald McDonald preached with such remarkable power. I look to the northward and see the district of Uigg, celebrate for the great number and proficiency of its first-class teachers, who persevere and step higher until they fill with honor and ability all the learned professions. A neat Baptist Church stands here founded by the late Rev. Samuel MacLeod, who in his pulpit exhortations, expressed "peace on earth", and led the way heavenward.

## ORWELL COVE

is a beautiful district, overlooking a charming bay. Many persons can yet remember when ships came here from England to load timber. The individual who could fill space in a ship's hold to the best advantage – the stevedore – was then the man of remarked importance. The labor enlivening chorus: Hi! ho! Cheerily men! Resounding so familiarly over and around the dimpling waters of Orwell Bay fifty years ago, is never heard now, its lingering echo having vanished with the fall of the last monarch birch. It was here that the Greenock ship *King David* in making preparations to load timber, with her sails loosed to dry, heeled over by a puff of wind and sank in seven fathoms of water. Several attempts were made to raise her, but all failed. A few years ago a wrecking company from Halifax endeavored to break her up for the great quantity of copper with which she was fastened, and although the most powerful explosives were used, so deep was she embedded in mud that they found the work unprofitable.

## ELDON.

A pretty village with everything brightly in its place, and a suitable place for a Baptist church, a graded school and a public hall.

## POINT PRIM.

In the years when we had a tariff for honest revenue, from this and adjacent districts came our shipmasters, officers and men, who by their physical endurance, energy and ability gave P.E. Island a bright dot on the map of the commercial world. I visit the place where Capt. Darby of the historic ship *Polly* disembarked passengers. Perhaps no ship ever conveyed across the Atlantic such a large number of strong, true, and brave men and women. The shore is not perceptibly changed, but the five hundred highlanders who landed here ninety-one years ago have all passed away "to the land of the leat." Some of them sleep in the old burial ground at Mt. Buchanan, but the large number are forever at rest in the beautiful cemetery of St. John's Presbyterian Church.

### PINETTE.

Two bridges span both branches of this river, and the streams which flow into it give power to saw more shingles and boards than are sawn in any other part of our Island.

### FLAT RIVER.

Why in the world don't they give this charming district a more flattering name? The scenery along its shady banks might then be set to music in harmony with its pastoral fields, and inviting homes, made such by the industry and skill of honest men and bonnie lasses.

### WOOD ISLANDS.

The north side of our Island has its many charms, but give me the south side where the balmy winds will roll the water over the red-brown sands as it does here, in luxuriant marmalade exuberance, and line the shores with bubbling foam, or by rocky headlands the bath lover can be showered with spray, and charmed by that far away, but impressive sound that has "music in its roar". On through Little Sands, and White Sands where at every home a highland welcome awaits the visitor to

### HIGH BANK.

True to its name, but well worthy of a more potential one. The road leads close by the shore from which you can enjoy a line view of the gull, dotted by the fishermen's boats.

M. C. R. Aug. 14, 1894.

[Published in *The Recaller*, May 1994.]

**William Stewart at Livingstone Cove, High Bank, 1941.** [Photo courtesy of Viola Gillis.]

# Chapter Six

꙳ᘐ

# The Sea

"During the days of sail, the more romantic and venturesome boys found an outlet for their energy at sea. They made brave, loyal and skilful seamen . . . many returned to the old parish to spend their declining years on or near the homestead on which they were born."
              - Malcolm MacQueen, *Hebridean Pioneers*.

**Captain Angus Young of Pinette**. While on voyage from Pictou to Pinette on November 2, 1884, the sails on Captain Young's schooner *Conqueror* tore. Captain Young went out on the main boom. He lost his balance, fell overboard, and drowned in the waters off of Flat River. He was 42 years of age. [Photo courtesy of Suzanne Dornbach, information courtesy of L. J. N. MacKenzie.]

# A Few of the Ships That Never Returned

*Angus McGowan*

In the summer of 1867, the full-rigged ship *Isabel*, owned by James Duncan and Co., commanded by Captain Alexander MacDonald, familiarly known as Sandy Hector of Point Prim, with Captain Roderick Cameron as mate. Cameron left her in Charlottetown. Donald MacAulay, also of Point Prim then went as mate and Simon M. Murchison, A. B. of Point Prim sailed with her. She came out from Glasgow and loaded oats here for New York. She arrived there in due time and discharged and loaded wheat for England. She sailed in good time and that was the last ever heard of her. Captain MacDonald was the grandfather of Mr. A. W. Hyndman of the Royal Bank, Charlottetown.

In 1868, the brig *Helen Davis*, commanded by Captain Jim Murchison, sailed from here bound for Barbados. Captain Murchison was also from Point Prim. The *Helen Davis* was loaded with a general cargo and a deck load of horses. She sailed from Charlottetown and that was the last ever heard of her.

The brig *Comet* sailed from Charlottetown in the fall of 1868, bound for Bermuda, with Captain Smith in command. The *Comet* was never heard of again.

In 1878, the new brigantine *Vigilant*, 475 tons, owned by Welch and Owens, sailed from Baltimore in September, loaded with wheat. She was commanded by Captain Malcolm MacLean of Belfast and there were with him second mate Peter Green, Martin O'Neill, and a colored cook, all belonging to the Island. The *Vigilant* was bound for Oporto, Portugal, but was never again heard from.

The barque *Assyrian*, 490 tons, owned by A. A. MacDonald Brothers, Georgetown, sailed from New York on February 6, 1878, commanded by Captain Murdoch Murchison of Point Prim. Three of his crew were Islanders: the Captain's brother John; Alexander MacDonald of Lyndale; and a Mr. Rice of Charlottetown. No tidings of vessel or crew ever reached the Island.

[Published in *The Recaller*, November 1987.]

---

"Many a ship sailed away manned from cabin-boy to master by a crew known to each other all their lives, and in many cases, near relations."

- Malcolm MacQueen, *Hebridean Pioneers*.

# Master Mariners From Belfast

*The Patriot*, 22 April 1922. Submitted by Joyce Kennedy.

No part of Prince Edward Island has given to the sea faring world so many master mariners as the grand old district of Belfast, as the following list will show:

- Capt. Alex Hector McDonald – Lost with all hands on the ship *Isabella*.
- Capt. Samuel McDonald – Died of fever at Charlottetown.
- Capt. Kenneth Finlayson – Died at Charlottetown of old age.
- Capt. William Finlayson – Lost overboard on a voyage to Africa.
- Capt. Sam McLean – Retired from sea.
- Capt. Roderick Cameron – Died at Charlottetown.
- Capt. Alex. Cameron – Died at Charlottetown.
- Capt. Donald M. McLeod – Died at Point Prim.
- Capt. Hector M. Murchison – Lost with all hands on an Ailas Bae steamer from New York to Cuba.

- Capt. Neil M. Murchison – Died at Vancouver.
- Capt. Murdock M. Murchison – Lost with all hands on the barque *Assyrian*, New York to London.
- Capt. Hector J. Murchison – Died of yellow fever in Venezuela.
- Capt. John J. Murchison – Last running the ferry at Borden and Cape Tormentine.
- Capt. Angus J. Murchison – Lost with all hands on the brig *Tantana*.
- Capt. Malcolm Murchison – Died of old age at North River.
- Capt. James Murchison – Lost with all hands on the brig *Helen Davis*, Charlottetown to Barbados.
- Capt. Peter Murchison – Died at Charlottetown.
- Capt. John James Murchison – Retired at Buenos Aires.
- Capt. Roderick Murchison – Died at San Francisco, California.
- Capt. Neil D. Murchison – Retired at San Rafael, Argentina.
- Capt. Peter D. Murchison – Died at San Francisco, California.
- Capt. Donald D. Murchison – Sailing six massed barkentine out of California, Australia and New Zealand.
- Capt. Martin McRae – Lost in the American ship *Samaria* with all hands.
- Capt. John McRae – Lost with ship *Anglo-India*. Some of the crew were saved on Formosa Island.
- Capt. Alex. McRae – Killed off a bridge in California.
- Capt. Samuel Nicholson – Lost on board his steamer off Sandy Hook.
- Capt. Malcolm Nicholson, Master of four massed full rigged ship *Simila*. She was cut in two in the English Channel while sailing from London to Calcutta. Crew were all saved.

- Capt. Donald A. McRae – Died at Point Prim.
- Capt. Murdock D. McRae – Died at Point Prim.
- Capt. Murdock R. McDonald – Drowned at Halifax.
- Capt. John Gillis – Died at Glasgow.
- Capt. Donald McRae – At Annandale.
- Capt. Samuel Buchanan – At Breadalbane.
- Capt. Alex McLeod – Died at Point Prim.
- Capt. Malcolm McLeod – Died of old age in Winnipeg.
- Capt. Peter Lockeman – Lost with all hands, except a cabin boy who floated away to sea on a piece of wreckage and picked up by a passenger ship – a four massed full rigger ship. She was lost near Madagascar.
- Capt. Malcolm Lockman – Died at Bermuda. Was last Superintendent of the Quebec Steamship Company, out of New York.
- Capt. Allan McAulay – Died at sea near San Francisco.
- Capt. Alex. McAulay – Died near Portland, Maine.
- Capt. Neil Campbell, Uigg – Killed by a passing train at Portland, while in the act of boarding his ship.
- Capt. Murdock McLeod, Orwell – Drowned in the Pacific Ocean.
- Capt. Roderick McLeod, Orwell – Died in Australia.
- Capt. Donald McLeod, Orwell – Died in Liverpool of smallpox.
- Capt. John C. Nicholson, Orwell – Died at Charlottetown.
- Capt. John A. Nicholson, Orwell – Retired on a farm.
- Capt. Duncan McDougall, Eldon – Retired on a farm.
- Capt. Alexander McLeod, Orwell – Died on his last ship, the *Northumberland.*
- Capt. John McLeod, Orwell – Died sailing out of New York.
- Capt. Neil McLeod, Orwell – Died at sea, Pacific Ocean.
- Capt. Angus McDougall, Eldon – Retired at Charlottetown.
- Capt. Archie McEachern, Eldon – Drowned at Brisbane, Australia.
- Capt. Allan Finlayson, Eldon – Retired at Charlottetown.
- Capt. Thomas Young, Pinette – Died in Pinette.
- Capt. Angus Young – Drowned off Belle River.
- Capt. Tom McRae – Died on Northumberland.
- Capt. David McRae – Died in New York.
- Capt. Malcolm McLeod (Rory) of Eldon.
- Capt. Rory McRae, Pinette – Died at Pinette of old age.
- Capt. Alex A. Campbell, Pinette – Died at New Zealand of old age.
- Capt. Roderick A. Campbell, Pinette – Frozen while crossing from Pictou to Wood Islands.
- Capt. Allan A. Campbell, Pinette – Drowned in the biggest English ship, the *Audroina,* then afloat. She was sailing from New York to Calcutta.
- Capt. A. Hector Campbell, Pinette – Lost with all hands on English full rigged ship from Bombay to Liverpool.
- Capt. Norman Campbell, Pinette – Sailing out of Liverpool.
- Capt. Dan McRae, Pinette – Superintendent at Edison, Chicago.

- Capt. Roderick McKenzie, Pinette – Died of old age.
- Capt. Alex Shaw, Pinette – Murdered at sea in bark *Veronica* from Mobile to Buenos Aires. All officers killed. Some of the crew were hung at Liverpool.
- Capt. John McPherson, Pinette – Died at Medicine Hat, Alberta.
- Capt. Malcolm McPherson, Pinette – Died in Western Canada.
- Capt. Hector Morrison, Pinette – Died in California.
- Capt. Malcolm McLean, Surrey – Lost with all hands on barkentine *Vigilant*, Baltimore to London.
- Capt. Angus Brown, Wood Islands – Died of old age at Wood Islands.
- Capt. Lachy McLean, Wood Islands – Living in Western States.
- Capt. William McLeod, Eldon – Lost overboard, P. E. Island to Liverpool.
- Capt. Dan McInnis, Pinette – Died of smallpox in the South Atlantic on the brig *Gleneairn*.
- Capt. Donald Hector McDonald – Died at Pinette.
- Capt. Donald Neil Murchison – Died at Point Prim.
- Capt. John McLean – Died at Point Prim.
- Capt. Murdock Finlayson – Retired.
- Capt. Donald D. McRae, Pinette – Died at Pinette.
- Capt. Rory A. McRae, Pinette – Retired on a farm in Pinette.
- Capt. J. McDougall of Belle River.
- Capt. John Riley of Belle River.
- Capt. Alex McInnis, Pinette – Retired on a farm at Pinette.
- Capt. Rory Nicholson, Orwell – Died Orwell.
- Capt. John McDonald, Orwell – Died Orwell.
- Capt. Archie Finlayson, Point Prim – Died at Point Prim of old age.

[Published in *The Recaller*, September 1998.]

---

## Fished up, at Rifleman's Rock

A SHIP'S ANCHOR, weighing about 10 cwt. (without a stock), with two shackles of chain thereto attached.

The owner is requested to come forward, prove property and pay expenses, otherwise they will be sold at Public Auction, at the subscriber's premises, on SATURDAY, the fourth day of OCT. next, at the hour of 12 o'clock, noon.

ANGUS McMILLAN.
Wood Islands, July 1st, 1867.

[Published in *The Recaller*, June 1994.]

# Drowning at Orwell Cove

*The Patriot*, June 25, 1895.

The horrifying intelligence was flashed over the wire this morning to *The Patriot*, of the accidental drowning of three men in the prime of life, in Orwell River, yesterday (Thursday) afternoon. The particulars received of the accident are as follows: -

At 2 o'clock in the afternoon James Daly, Edmund Hughes, and John Hughes[1] were gathering oysters on the shore off the farm at Orwell lately owned and occupied by Norman MacLeod, of J. D. MacLeod & Co., of this city. Afterwards it is supposed that Edmund Hughes went in swimming, and after getting beyond his depth commenced to sink. The other two, seeing his danger, bravely went to his rescue and perished in the attempt to save him. This supposition is strengthened by the fact that Edmund Hughes' body was nude when recovered, and the others were partly dressed.

The father of the two deceased boys, James Hughes, now owns and occupies Mr. MacLeod's farm, and it seems that his little child, a boy aged eight, went to the shore and seeing his brother's clothes on the bank went home and told his parents.

**Gravestone of Edmund and John Hughes, St. Michael's, Iona.** [Photo courtesy of L. J. N. MacKenzie.]

[Published in *The Recaller*, June 1993.]

Thoroughly alarmed, the parents with some neighbors hastened to the shore where they found Edmund's clothes and some other things belonging to the three men. A boat was procured and the water and shore in that vicinity thoroughly searched with the result of finding the three stalwart men who had gone out that afternoon in the full vigor of manly strength, cold in death.

Last evening, James St. Croix Moore, Esq., Coroner, held an inquest, when a verdict of "accidental death by drowning" was returned.

[1] According to Father Arthur O'Shea, *It Happened in Iona*, James Daly had just completed his third year at medical school in Halifax. Edmund and John Hughes were his cousins.

# Strait Talk

*Dr. Stewart MacDonald*

Sixty years ago, not all fishermen used expensive wharves and breakwaters to moor their boats. They fashioned what were known as *killicks,* which were made by cutting a hole in a large stone and putting it over quite a large tree which had its roots left on to hold the stone in place. They sank this in deep water, preferably inside a bar on which the large waves break. When they tied their boat to the killick, the boat rode with the waves. I never heard of a boat swamping (filling with water) even in the worst storms.

Alex Blue fished and farmed, only three farms from my home in Little Sands. Occasionally, I went out with him to try and catch some cod fish. It gave me an idea of how hard these men worked for a living.

I remember going to Pictou with Alex Blue many years ago. A heavy fog had settled in. Just when Alex figured he was in the area of Pictou, he stopped the boat. We could hear fishermen working in the distance. The other passenger in the boat, Johnnie Blue, was an experienced seaman who had sailed around the world. Upon hearing the voices he called out, "Where is Pictou harbour?" And the call came back, "Is that you Johnnie Blue?" To that Johnnie replied, "Is that you McMaster?" (Blue and McMaster had been shipmates on the *Pinto*, which had been delivered to Russia during the First World War.) McMaster directed, "Steer straight west, you are at the mouth of the harbour."

That evening when we left for home, the last place we saw was the wharf in Pictou. We were unable to see the banks of the river due to the dense fog.

Alex Blue had a dollar watch and a compass. After we had sailed out of Pictou Harbour for exactly one hour, Alex set a course which he considered to be true north. After what seemed like hours in the dense fog that shrouded everything, Alex and Johnnie thought that we might be getting near land. They would stop the boat and sound for bottom, and they would shout in order to measure the distance to the shore line by the return echo. Alex put the boat into very slow speed, and the next thing we saw was his own killick, right ahead of him! I can say that I have never seen better navigation. But, I sometimes wonder if it was luck or pluck that enabled those early fishermen to find their way home in that heavy fog.

[Published in *The Recaller,* April 1996.]

# We Remember Charlie Lutz
## 1874 - 1968
*Hesta MacDonald*

*"Let not ambition mock their useful toil"*.
— Gray.

As a young boy only eight years of age, Charlie Lutz went to sea on the square riggers, now long gone from use, but in the days of sail, a much-used design.

Charlie used to relate an incident that occurred when he was a very young boy. He was ordered to scale one of the tall masts during a sharp gale at sea. With the ship tossing in the waves, he was unable to unfurl the top sail. After several futile efforts, he looked down to see one of the sailors ascending the mast, a knife held grimly in his teeth. "I'll show you once," the sailor told him, "but, if I have to come up here a second time, either you or I are going to hit that deck." Charlie made sure to learn the first time.

Charlie never forgot a voyage with a captain from Lunenburg, Nova Scotia. They called at Cuba, where they took on three crew men. During the voyage, one of the Cubans killed another. The captain said, "If there's any killing on this boat, I do the killing." The Cuban sailor was stripped and tied to the mast. The crew had to watch as the captain beat him with a rope. When the sailor was cut down, he collapsed on the deck. The captain kicked him into the sea and they sailed on.

Life was rigorous, discipline was harsh, and the occupation was hazardous. Charlie would tell about a time they were fishing whales on the Amazon River, when one of the gigantic mammals crashed right through the wood ship. As the ship was sinking, the crew members launched the small dory, where they survived the next two weeks until they were picked up.

After Charlie Lutz abandoned life as a seaman, he returned home where he lived out his ninety-and-some years, earning a living by fishing lobsters and as a woodsman. He lost one eye in a woods accident, but three months later he went back to work in the woods. It was a frosty day and on the first stroke of the axe, a chip flew up and struck his good eye. He had to sit on a stump for a long time until his vision cleared enough for him to find his way home. Dr. Lester Brehaut was called from Murray River. The doctor kept Charlie's eye bandaged for three weeks, and when the bandages were removed, he could see again.

**Charlie Lutz (right) with his wife Hannah and their great grandson Ronnie Moore, 1937.** [Photo courtesy of Clarence Moore.]

Charlie was tough in regard to his physical health. When the doctor diagnosed pneumonia, there were no "wonder drugs" and it looked as if he was going to die. Not so! Next day, Charlie was in the fishing boat with his son-in-law Edwin MacKenzie. When Charlie fell into the water among floating ice cakes, Edwin tried to persuade him to go ashore, but Charlie insisted on finishing the day's task.

When Charlie died in his late nineties, a post mortem examination revealed an old heart attack with a large area of old scar tissue. Charlie had never known that he had heart trouble and had never missed a day's work because of it. Charlie was a good citizen and a superb storyteller.

[Published in *The Recaller*, June 1994.]

ON Friday night last Messrs. Murdock Morrison, Hector D. McKenzie, Roderick D. Reid, Daniel McLean, Robert McWilliams and Angus Finlayson – all active and intelligent young men from Eldon and Flat River – took passage in the *St. Lawrence* for Shediac on their way to Virginia City, in Nevada, United States, where they intend to prosecute their fortunes for a few years. We wish them success, and shall always be glad to hear from them.

- June 12, 1873.

[Published in *The Recaller*, June 1994.]

# Memories of a Fisherman's Daughter

*Joyce Livingstone Kennedy*

When I was a child, I remember we spent our winters preparing for the fishing season. Saplings were cut to make trap bows. I loved when my father bent the bows. . . I can still remember the fragrant smell of the wood in steaming water. Traps were built. Papers were laid in the bottom of the trap and cement was poured in for ballast. Flat stones were also used.

"Knitting heads" was a family affair, with my good-natured, patient father allowing even little ones to help. Of course, after the little one had gone to bed, he had the task of undoing all the tangles and knots. However, we eventually learned to knit heads properly, and this was an evening chore we all enjoyed. I used to like to knit with the needles my father had carved out himself. He was very resourceful, even building his own boats with the help of his nephew Raymond MacLean.

Around April 22$^{nd}$ each year, we would be off to Wood Islands, leaving our comfortable home in High Bank to live in a two room shanty for the duration of the fishing season. We would leave in the early morning, before the dirt roads had thawed out. Some years were worse than others for mud. My brother Ronnie remembers the road below Jimmie Dixon's in Little Sands being so bad that they had to leave the road and travel through the field. My only memory of this is sitting in the cab of Rollie MacPherson's truck, being terrified that we would be stuck in the mud forever. We were the last to get through the Shore Road that spring, everyone else had to go around by other roads to reach Wood Islands.

Our shanty was on the side of the road where the ferry parking lot is now located. One night there was a terrible storm, with heavy winds and rain. Not only was the water rising outside the shanty, but inside as well. I remember my father carrying us, wading through the water, to the road. We went to Ken Beck's shanty on the Burma Road to wait for my uncle, Dr. Stewart MacDonald who was coming to take us up to Papa's (my grandfather's).

Sometime after this, our shanty was moved to the Burma Road. There, we had an even smaller shanty that the hired man had previously stayed in. Other families who stayed there for the season included Percy Richards, Archie Gamble, Ken Beck, and Henry Richards. For fresh water, we used the pump at Alex Young's, and sometimes we went to Angus Brown's for milk.

It seemed that each boat in the harbour had its own characteristics. My brother Ronnie could tell whose boat was coming through the entrance by the sound of the engine. I could only recognize Archie Gamble's boat, because it had a very distinct sound.

The fishermen used to sell to "the smacks". These were fish buyers who traveled around from port to port, often by boats, and later by trucks. Two such buyers were Jack Gillis and Harry Streight. Later I remember Nicholson's coming with a big truck. They would weigh the crates of lobsters and take the "canners" to the factory at Belle River. The "market" size lobsters were shipped away live.

Life in the shanties must have been hectic for the wives, but for us children it was a great time, as we could renew old friendships and play. In the early years, play at the shore was filled with warnings to never touch anything strange looking, but to immediately tell an adult. Even though we were young, we knew all this had something to do with the war. Often we would find things like canned goods washed up on the shore. Most of these would be canned beans, which we would stir into mudpies.

1951 was the last summer we lived at the shore in Wood Islands. After that, my father traveled back and forth from home to the wharf. I missed going to the shore, but times and things had changed.

I can still see my father, after days of bad weather had kept the boats on shore, standing in the doorway of our High Bank home on a Sunday morning, watching other fishermen hauling their traps. He would remark, "We're given six days to work and this is not one of them. For the sake of a few lobsters it's not worth breaking the Sabbath."

I wouldn't trade those happy, fun-filled days of being a fisherman's daughter for anything.

[Published in *The Recaller*, April 1996.]

**Wood Islands Wharf.** [Photo courtesy of Tommy and Dora MacKenzie.]

# Rum-running in the 1920's

*Dr. Stewart MacDonald*

When I attended school in Little Sands, it was quite common to see schooners laid off the shores of the Island. These schooners brought many loads of rum to our shores in the 1920's. Conditions were very much different from today. Very few people had cars and travel was difficult due to the condition of the highways. The roads were dirt roads, often with a band of grass growing along the middle portion.

In the heyday of rum running, it was not uncommon to hear a truck going by late at night after the household was in bed. Then, we always said, "There goes another load of rum". At that time it was selling for five dollars a gallon or two dollars a bottle. Many people drove to White Sands and bought a five gallon barrel for twenty five dollars.

Many tricks were used to circumvent the law. Several small boats would unload the cargo of rum from a schooner off Murray Harbour, well outside the three-mile limit. When all were loaded, the fastest boats would take off in different directions, leading the police patrol boats a merry chase, while the other boats safely landed their rum on shore. The fast boats soon outstripped the police and headed safely for their selected destination.

The rum runners put mufflers on the motors of their boat engines, but we soon learned to recognize the muffled purr of their engines as they skirted the shore during the night.

A certain amount of craft was used by the boat captains to lure the provincial police away from the spot where a large shipment of rum was to be landed. The story is told of one captain who bought a barn from a minister. The minister's conscience bothered him after the sale, so he went to town and reported it. The result was that all the provincial police were lying in wait to catch the rumrunners, while the crafty bootleggers, knowing the minister would report them, unloaded their cargo elsewhere and transported it safely to Charlottetown for ready sale.

In that era of the late twenties, there was great fear of the boats that sailed up and down the Northumberland Strait staying safely out beyond the three-mile limit. So, in 1926, the Dominion Government passed a law that Established the Northumberland Strait as inland waters. This greatly limited the rum running in the southern part of Prince Edward Island.

[Published in *The Recaller*, September 1986.]

# Chapter Seven

❧

# Military Service

"I am going to the War," he said.

"Are you going to-night or in the morning?" I asked him.

"It will be a long war," he answered, "and I don't think they will miss me much if I wait until morning."

- Sir Andrew MacPhail, *The Master's Wife*.

**The World War I monument at St. John's Presbyterian Church Cemetery.** [Photo courtesy of L. J. N. MacKenzie.]

---

# World War I Monument
# St. John's Church Cemetery

The following information is engraved on the war monument in St. John's Presbyterian Church Cemetery:

Sacred to the
imperishable Memory
of our
heroic sons
who gave their
lives in the
World War.
1914-1918.

Angus MacDonald,
Born Sept. 2, 1888,
Killed at St. Eloi,
Apr. 4, 1916.

Allan N. MacDonald,
Born 1899,
Killed in France 1916,

Frederick S. Halliday,
Born 1888,
Killed in Action,
at Somme,
Nov. 16, 1916.

Frederick Martin,
Born July 8, 1890,
Died in England,
Oct. 22, 1916.

Alexander R. MacRae,
Born Nov. 1895,
Killed in Action,
at Vimy Ridge,
Apr. 9, 1917.

John H. MacTavish,
Born Apr. 12, 1888,
Killed in Action at
Passchendaele,
Oct. 30, 1917.

Robert A. Anderson,
Born Apr. 6, 1896,
Died Jan. 14, 1918.

John M. Murchison,
Born June 11, 1896,
Killed at Amiens,
Aug. 8, 1918.

Whitney Martin,
Born Dec. 2, 1896,
Died at Amiens,
Aug. 26, 1918.

Neil Ross,
Born March 22, 1894,
Killed at Cherisy,
Aug. 28, 1918.

Albert H. Gaucher,
Born 1887,
Died Sept. 7, 1918.

A. Sinclair
MacKenzie,
Born May 27, 1891,
Killed in Action at
Cambrai,
Oct. 10, 1918.

Roderick Enman,
Born 1896,
Died in Ch.town,
May 1917.

John W. MacLeod,
Born July 6, 1886,
Died May 9, 1917.

Lauchlin MacLeod,
Born May 1889,
Killed at
Passchendaele,
Oct. 31, 1917.

Murdock Matheson
Born 1892, Killed at
Passchendaele,
Nov. 10, 1917.

Ernest J. Rockwell,
Born Aug. 26, 1898,
Died in England
Jan. 31, 1917.

"Greater love hath no
man than this."

[Published in *The Recaller*,
October 1993.]

---

# Memorial Day in Belfast

In common with many other places, the 19th of July was duly observed by the people of Belfast as Memorial Day of the end of the Great War. The gathering took place on the historic church grounds, and was numerously attended. Many notable persons and visitors from abroad added to the day's pleasure. The ladies had brought full baskets and long tables were duly served. No place could be more suitable for such an assembly than just that spot.

So far as we know no community had a more compelling reason for celebrating the event of peace than the district of Belfast. Nearly, if not all, of one hundred young men born and brought up here heard and readily answered their country's call. Thirteen of their number are now asleep in "Flanders Field".

Some $4,000 was collected by the societies and $700 was spent in welcoming the boys on their return. A resolution was passed to put up a suitable memorial monument to the memory of the boys who made the supreme sacrifice.

Rev. J. W. MacKenzie took charge and called upon Mr. Malcolm MacKenzie, elder, to introduce a distinguished Belfaster, ex-Governor MacKinnon. Mr. MacKinnon delivered a speech about the things well worth remembering about our country, the war, and the noble Belfast boys. Then, Mr. Alexander Martin, ex-M.P. made a fine address which the people were glad to hear.

Near the close of the day, advantage was taken of the occasion to celebrate another event. It was discovered that the induction of the present pastor, synchronized with the peace settlement, on the 19th of July nine years ago.

The program ended with solos and patriotic airs closing with the National Anthem.

ONE WHO WAS PRESENT.

[Published in *The Recaller*, November 1997.]

---

### Killed in Action: Private John McTavish

Mrs. Donald MacTavish, Newtown, Belfast has received a telegraph informing her that her son Private John Hector McTavish is officially reported killed in action on October 30th, 1917. Private McTavish, who was a contractor, has been in the western states for the past 10 years and enlisted on December 5th at Edmonton with the 138th.

# The Military Will of John W. McLeod

*Linda Jean Nicholson MacKenzie*

Considering the number of Island men who fought and died in World War I, it is surprising that few military wills were filed with the P.E.I. Probate Court. Of the hundreds of estates filed between 1914 and 1918, only seven persons were identified as "military men". One of these was John William McLeod of Pinette.

In 1905, John William McLeod was listed in *The Patriot* newspaper as one of many Islanders leaving for western Canada during the Harvest Excursions. Born in Glasbhein on July 6, 1886, he was the son of Angus McLeod and Katherine McRae. He was only 19 years old when he left the Island.

It appears John intended to stay in western Canada, as he purchased a parcel of property in Fort William, Ontario. But, when World War I began, he joined the 46th Battalion and was sent overseas.

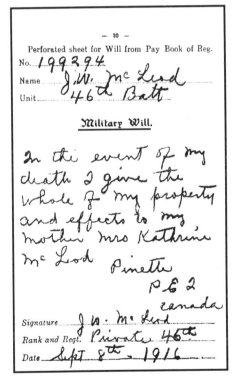

**The Military Will of John William McLeod.** Estates Division of the Supreme Court, Charlottetown, PEI, File No. 1013, Book 20, Page 478.

On September 8, 1916, Private John McLeod executed his last will and testament. Like many of his fellow soldiers, he utilized a blank Military Will printed in his Pay Book. In his will, John bequeathed all of his property to his mother, Mrs. Katherine McLeod of Pinette.

John William McLeod died on May 9, 1917 of wounds received in France. In September 1917, his mother applied to the Prince Edward Island Probate Court for administration of his estate. Her petition stated that her son was insured with Prudential Insurance Company for one thousand dollars and that he owned property in western Canada. She said her son had made a will, but she did not have it in her possession. Several days later the will was forwarded to Misters

McLean and McKinnon, Barristers of Charlottetown. It was brought before the court and proved on the oaths of Leonard B. Miller of Charlottetown, Principal of Charlottetown Business College, and Malcolm A. McLeod of Pinette, Farmer, who swore they were familiar with the handwriting of John McLeod, and in their opinions, he had written and signed the will. The court granted an Administration cum testamento annexo ("with the will annexed") to Katherine McLeod and recorded the military will of Private John William McLeod in Record Book 20.

[Published in *The Recaller*, October 2000.]

---

# Killed in Action: Lieutenant Nicholson

The following letter has been received by Miss Jessie Nicholson, sister of the late Lieut. Angus Nicholson, who was killed in action in France on March 6th, 1918:

France, 7th March 1918

Dear Miss Nicholson,

I am just sending you a few lines of sympathy on the death of your brother, Angus and to give you more details how he met his death, than you received in the official telegram.

Your brother, Angus, went out on patrol on the night of the 6th of March for the purpose of inspecting our wire. The enemy machine gunners were rather active at the time, but Angus was always so awfully keen to do his duty, that he took the chance on getting away from the machine gunners, but unfortunately he was hit twice, he did not suffer any pain, as he was hit through the head. I was greatly upset when I heard he was missing, as he was a most efficient and keen officer and a great comrade and will be greatly missed in the Company. I have his wrist watch and pocket book, -- the same I shall send to you at the first opportunity, by registered mail. If there is anything I can possibly due for you with regards in information you would like to know – please call on me, as I shall be only too pleased to oblige.

I shall close now, sending my sincere sympathy to all his friends, I remain.
Yours sincerely,
Lieutenant D. Clellard,
No. 4 Co 16th Canadian Scottish Brigade.

Lieutenant Nicholson was the son of Capt. J. A. Nicholson, Orwell Cove.

[Published in *The Recaller*, October 1993.]

---

**Soldiers Monument at Orwell Head.**

Erected by Orwell Head Congregation in memory of our heroic dead.
Who gave their lives in defense of home and country.

1914-1919
1939-1945

L. Corp. Everett McLeod, 1893-1916.
Sgt. A. Pope Nicholson, 1894-1916.
Malcolm McDonald, 1892-1917.
Alexander McDonald, 1888-1917.
John C. Martin, 1895-1919.
Sgt. J. Samuel Nicholson, M. M., 1898-1918.
Wellington D. Enman, 1892-1918.
Wallace C. McLeod, 1895-1918.
John C. McLeod, 1898-1918.
Corp. Monty J. McLeod, 1890-1918.
John W. Martin, 1896-1919.
E. Stanley McLeod, 1902-1943.
Flt. Sgt. Kimble C. Saunderson, 1923-1943.
F/O Donald W. Hume, 1921-1944.
Ewen A. McLeod, 1925-1944.

"Greater love hath no man than this,
that a man lay down his life for his friends."

---

**George E. Docherty.**
Born March 9, 1897, the youngest son of John and Mary Docherty, George joined the Canadian Army at the age of 17 as a Canadian Guard. On September 18, 1916, he went overseas with the 85th Battalion of the Nova Scotia Highlanders. He was wounded in the neck on September 27, 1918 in Cambrai, France and was left for dead. After the battle, Colonel J. L. Ralston found George and helped transport him to a Military Hospital. George named his third son James Layton Ralston Docherty after the Colonel who saved his life. [Photo courtesy of Esther Mutch. Information courtesy of Layton Docherty.]

*The Past is Before Us*

# The Island of Red Clay

*George MacPherson*

Back there on P.E. Island
At a place called Beach Grove Inn,
It was there that I volunteered to fight
For my country and my king.

I knew my country needed me,
So I volunteered to go
And to my friends around Belfast
I bade them Au Revoir.

I bade farewell to neighbours kind,
My friends and sisters gay,
And my father's farm where I was born,
On the shores of Orwell Bay.

It was there I spent my golden youth
No worldly cares had I,
Till the clouds of war cast shadows
On good old P.E.I.

The army was recruiting
And I was young and free,
So I joined up with the Islander
In the Second R.C.A.

I left behind those neighbours kind
My friends and sisters gay,
And my father's farm where the salt sea breezes,
Sweep in from the Orwell Bay.

Although between me and my friends
The broad Atlantic lay,
Yet memories always take me back
To the Island of Red Clay.

[Published in *The Recaller*, November 1994.]

# We Remember Them
*Mary Ross*

## A. Ross MacPherson
### March 8, 1916 – July 11, 1992

Born on March 8, 1916, Ross was the son of Malcolm George MacPherson and his wife Elizabeth (nee MacNeill).

**Ross and his "War Bride" Ann.** [Photo courtesy of Auldene MacKenzie.]

Ross enlisted in the armed forces in 1939, at the very beginning of the hostilities. He served in England with the West Nova Scotia Regiment, before fighting in Italy, where he was wounded.

After convalescence in England, he continued military service there until 1947. Returning to Canada in January 1947, he received his honorable discharge later that year.

[Information obtained from Ross's widow, Ann MacPherson.]

## Neil Archibald Murchison
### December 3, 1913 – September 8, 1944

Neil Archibald Murchison was born in Point Prim on December 3, 1913. He was the son of the late Donald Neil Murchison and Sarah Nicholson Murchison.

There was a call to arms issued by the Canadian Government before the war was declared. Neil joined the army on September 1, 1939. Others who enlisted at that time were Ross MacPherson from Eldon, Joe Saunders from Point Prim, and John D. MacKinnon from Mount Buchanan.

Neil went overseas with the North Nova Scotia Highlanders in the fall of 1941. He went into France during the height of the war and was killed near Coen on September 8, 1944.

Neil's brother, Manson, was with the army in Italy at the time of his brother's death. Their sister Aggie's letter with the news of Neil's death did not reach Manson for two months. At this time Manson was in an Italian hospital nursing a bad leg wound.

Neil died for the principles he believed in. We will honor and remember him always.

[Information obtained from Manson Murchison.]

## John D. MacKinnon
### March 12, 1916 – April 19, 1991

John D. MacKinnon of Mount Buchanan was born on March 12, 1916, the son of Dougald and Mary Sarah "Mamie" (MacWilliams) MacKinnon. He was among the first to respond to Canada's call to arms at the outbreak of World War II when he enlisted in the Prince Edward Island Highlanders on September 4, 1939.

John transferred to D. Company, Cape Breton Highlanders on March 16, 1943, and embarked for overseas duty on April 10th of the same year.

After 29 months overseas, John returned to Canada on September 24, 1945 and received an honorable discharge on October 25, 1945.

During 74 months of active military service, John served in Italy, England, the Mediterranean, and northwestern Europe.

[Information provided by John's widow, Willena MacKinnon. See also "We Remember Dougald MacKinnon" written about John's father. ]

## Winsor Kennedy
### March 24, 1924 – March 13, 1993

Winsor Kennedy was born in Iris, Prince Edward Island, on March 24, 1924, the son of Joe and Frances (MacLeod) Kennedy. He joined the army on April 1, 1943, just after his nineteenth birthday.

Winsor was a dispatcher with the Signal Corps. R.C.C.S., and served in Canada and Europe.

On March 4, 1946, Winsor returned home, but he continued to serve for three years with the Royal Canadian Dragoons.

During his last years, Winsor lived in Flat River, where he was an active and highly valued member of the community. He devoted time and talents to the Community Schools, and was an active member of the Royal Canadian Legion in Halifax, Nova Scotia and Eldon, P.E.I.

[Information provided by family members.]

[Published in *The Recaller,* November 1997.]

# We Remember Jean I. Morrison
## 1912 - 1995
*Hesta MacDonald*

Jean I. MacKenzie was born in Flat River on October 31, 1912, and received her early education in the local school. Then, at the age of 16 years, she left home to pursue her studies at Mt. Allison University where she spent the next two years.

The next move was to Montreal, where Jean trained for three years at the Royal Victoria Hospital. After graduation as a nurse, she continued work at that hospital. Later, she went to Vancouver, where she nursed at St. Vincent's Hospital.

**Jean MacKenzie in uniform.** [Photo courtesy of Donald MacKenzie.]

Then, it was on to Bralorne, about 150 miles north of Vancouver. It was there that Jean enlisted as a nurse in the Canadian Army. She served for two years in the Polar Bear force, in which she was one of only two nurses who, along with one surgeon (Dr. George Dewar), made up a field hospital unit.

At that time, the war with Japan was being fought, and it was feared the Japanese might invade the Canadian Arctic. For that reason, Polar Bear was training troops and testing equipment for arctic warfare. Testing clothing was part of the objective. Dr. George Dewar in his book *Prescription for a Full Life*, describes how the Polar Bear bivouacked in sub-zero temperatures using only tents or spruce boughs as shelter. . . a sure way to determine what clothing is most effective against arctic temperatures!

Following an honorable discharge after the war, Jean returned home in 1946. She married Hector Morrison and devoted herself to making a happy home. Two children, Allan and Sheila, made up the family. Jean also took an active part in the community, as long as her health permitted.

Jean Morrison died on February 7, 1995. We, in the Belfast Historical Society, are proud to salute Jean Morrison, her contribution to her country as an Army Nurse, and as a good citizen in the Belfast community.

[Published in *The Recaller*, June 1995.]

# Belfasters Recall

## Dr. Stewart MacDonald,

Flying Officer in World War II recalls: -

As a navigator in the R.C.A.F., I was part of the air crew of a bomber squadron. Twenty times we flew into the Ruhr Valley, the great industrial heartland of Hitler's war production. To air crews, the Ruhr was known as "Happy Valley", ironically enough, for hundreds of aircraft were lost there. The flak [antiaircraft fire] there was terrible!

On October 30, 1944, we were briefed to bomb Cologne (Koln) in the Ruhr, one of four times I logged bombing raids there. On this night, when our bombs were released, the Bomb Aimer called to alert us that the "block-buster" (a 4,000 pound bomb) was frozen to our plane – right below the navigation desk. While we waited for the explosion that would end our careers, the pilot headed to the north, sending our craft into a series of swift dives and sharp upward curves. After four or five of those maneuvers, we were overjoyed to hear the Bomb Aimer's voice, "Bombs gone!"

Next morning the report came that one of the crews had dropped a load of bombs on a bridge over the Rhine, and had utterly destroyed it. We knew what had happened to the bridge, as it was directly north from Cologne. But, having been sent to bomb Cologne, we knew it would not be prudent to admit that we were bombing elsewhere. So, we kept silent!

Thirty years later, I was reading a book by the American economist John Kenneth Galbraith, who had gone to Europe to study the effect of the war. I was startled to read his opinion that "the most useful damage of any bomb dropped in the war was dropped by a crew that had missed the target of Cologne, knocking out a bridge on the Rhine, thereby stopping traffic on the river for a month."

I checked my log book. Sure enough, the date was confirmed. At once I phoned my pilot, Ken Roulston, in Ottawa, and we agreed that we no longer had to keep our secret of how we shook off the block-buster.

[Published in *The Recaller*, October 1993.]

## Albert MacDonald,

Who was with the Royal Canadian Navy in World War II recalls: -

While escorting a convoy, on the triangle run from New York to Halifax to St. John's, Newfoundland, in the North Atlantic of St. John's, we would meet another escort that would take the convoy overseas. Around 2 am one morning, we heard reports of submarines in the area.

For some reason, in the very dense fog and with no lights on any of the ships, we found ourselves in the middle of the convoy. Suddenly, a big freighter loomed up out of the fog and hit our mine sweeper broadside. It sliced the left side of the bridge off. For reasons unknown to us and by the grace of God, we escaped further damage and got away from the convoy. The next day, we were able to sail back to St. John's under our own power. After several weeks in repairs, we got back to dry-dock in Halifax.

[Published in *The Recaller*, October 1993.]

## Malcolm Nicholson

Who served with the Army's Signal Corp. in World War II recalls: -

The most meaningful church service I ever attended was in a field outside Coen in France while the sound of shells bursting in the distance could be heard.

[Published in *The Recaller*, October 1993.]

# A Letter From the Front

The following letter, written by Private John A. MacLeod of Pinette, was very typical of letters sent home from the front. Rarely did these brave men make mention of the danger that was their constant companion. Only a month after this letter was written, Private MacLeod was killed in action.

July 9th 1944 #2 C.B.R.G.

Dear Brother,

Received the thousand cigarettes you sent me just got them in time was completely out of cigarettes, received the parcel the same day. The cake is very good, I don't mind telling you I'm not very struck on the pipe you sent me.

I met Murdock and Lloyd last Sunday and Murdock and Eugene again last night. They haven't changed any, was certainly glad to see them, Murdock said he saw everybody that came over here from around home, except Malcolm Nicholson and Jack Gillis.

Well, I'm in France now, and it's the first time I ever wished I could speak French. Well, there isn't anything exciting to write about, so hope to hear from some of you soon.

Love to all, John

[Published in *The Recaller,* October 1993.]

# Man of Many Awards

Feb. 13, 1946 – George Stewart of Wood Islands, P.E.I., the army sergeant who won the military medal 100 times but was awarded it only once, has been discharged from the Canadian Army after five years of the toughest war service that any Canadian has seen.

Sergeant-Major Stewart went "in" with the North Nova Scotia Highlanders on D-Day as a private, and quickly rose through the ranks to lance corporal, section commander, and platoon sergeant. In the fighting through Normandy to Germany, he lost many platoon commanders and took command of a platoon. At the end of the war, he found himself one of the "one" handful of North Novas who survived in a rifle platoon from D-Day without being killed or wounded. In that period he rose from buck private to sergeant major of "Charlie" Company.

Sergeant-Major Stewart began his army service with the Prince Edward Island Highlanders in Dartmouth in the winter of 1939 and went overseas to join the famed North Novas, which later came under the command of Col. D. F. Forbes. His name, known to thousands of men overseas, is highly revered in his battalion. Last December, Sergeant Major Stewart was commanded to appear before King George VI, to be awarded a medal.

Today, George Stewart who saw the toughest of infantry hand to hand fighting from the beaches of Normandy to the final capitulation of Germany still lives. He attributes his staying power and life to "just pure luck and common horse sense."

**George Stewart at the Wood Islands Lighthouse.** [Photo courtesy of Jean Stewart.]

[Published in *The Recaller*, November 1997.]

# We Salute David S. Ross

*Mary Ross*

On July 2, 1940, David Sinclair Ross of Eldon enlisted in the North Nova Scotia Highlanders. A young man of 29 years, Dave arrived in England on May 12, 1941, after training in Amherst, Nova Scotia. Letters and postcards sent to Dave's mother, Mrs. Charlotte Ross remain treasured family memorabilia. They also tell the story of David's military service.

In a letter dated August 17, 1944, Mrs. Ross was advised that her son Corporal David Ross was missing in action. She would later discover that on July 19, 1944 Dave had been taken prisoner near Coen, France by Nazi forces. In a telegram received on August 23, 1944, the Department of Defense informed Mrs. Ross that Dave was a prisoner of war in Germany.

Postcards from Dave, dated at two month intervals, conveyed only the message that he was well. But, after ten long months, Dave's mother received the following letter: "Dear Mother, I was recaptured by the Americans on April 30th and expect to be back in England by the end of the week. I am quite well and gaining back some weight I lost on the march from Poland, which started on Jan'y 23rd. We have been getting Red Cross parcels the past couple of weeks and are eating and smoking more, than since I was captured. I don't know how long I will be in England. I would like to stay a couple of weeks to see some friends and then they can't send me home soon enough. I have not heard or received any mail since November, but hope you and all the rest are in good health. Will see you soon, so get cooking. Love, David."

After returning home, in a statement to the War Claims Commission concerning a claim for maltreatment, Dave wrote the following: "On the morning of 23 January '45, I came out of sick bay in Work Camp E902 and marched to Ratilon, a distance of 50 miles in 24 hours. And from there we went to my final destination. We marched every day for the first month, and then until April 23 we marched two days and rested one, except for a brief period at Regensburg, where we were sent to work clearing debris from the station area where we were caught in two bombing raids."

In another paper, which appears to be personal notes to himself, Dave recorded his experiences of poor and insufficient food, lack of sanitation, prevalence of illness and disease during the 800 mile march.

Dave Ross returned to Eldon, where he operated the family business until his death at the young age of 49 years in 1960.

[Published in *The Recaller*, November 1994.]

# Chapter Eight

❧❧

# Progress

"The prosperity of a country depends on water and the quality of its soil, as well as the character of its people. . . Belfast has been blessed with good grass and good people."

— Malcolm MacQueen, *Hebridean Pioneers.*

**Murdock and Mary MacRae at Point Prim.** [Photo courtesy of Stewart and Barbara MacRae.]

# Horsepower

*Hesta MacDonald*

The horse stable on Island farms is now decrepit, or gone altogether. Yet, only a few decades ago, horses were a valuable asset whose hard work made possible the prosperity of the farming communities.

Farmers relied on their horses for ploughing, harrowing, seeding, haying, and harvesting. As years brought new equipment, horses helped with jobs previously done by manual labour. For example, the horse-drawn hay mower released the farmer from the long and strenuous task of mowing the fields by scythe.

**Clarence Gillis (on the hay), Mary Gillis (in the barn) and friend, ca. 1940.** [Photo courtesy of Eliza Gillis.]

A horse was especially useful during the haying operation in lifting the hay into the barn loft using a special hay fork. One member has described it this way: "The coiled hay was taken up to the barn by truck wagon. The barn loft was fitted with a carrier (a long beam with rails like a railroad on either side). The hay fork was attached to a sliding carriage (mounted on the railed beam described above), and a horse was hitched to a "swing", a series of ropes and pulleys designed to lower and raise the big fork, and move the carriage along the beam inside the barn loft. The man or woman in charge, at a signal from the person on the load, put the fork into the hay on the load and locked it. When he got the go-ahead signal, he started the horse pulling it into the loft. When it was over the appropriate spot in the loft, the worker on the load tripped the fork and dropped the hay into the loft."

Potatoes being a major crop, horses helped with laying out the drills, covering the seed, spraying for bugs and blight, and in the hauling of the potatoes to the cellar for storage. From time to time during the growing season, the potatoes were "scuffled". This appears to be an Island term, and it is defined in *The Dictionary of Prince Edward Island English*, compiled by T. K. Pratt. He says: "When at length the potato patch became large enough to be called a field, a kind of horse-drawn scuffler was made by the farmer to supplement the hoe which was still used to build up drills around the plants."

**Gordon and Frances MacDonald and friends, ca. 1949, delivering grain to the field.**
[Photo courtesy of Viola Gillis.]

Hauling seaweed and mussel mud to be used as fertilizer on the fields was yet another chore carried out with the help of the horse.

The major task of the winter months was getting out the wood in sufficient quantity to last the next long, cold, bitter winter. The process of hauling logs out of the woodlots was called "twitching" logs, another Island term defined by Pratt. In his book *It Happened in Iona*, Rev. Art O'Shea describes travelling to the woodlot by horse and wood sleigh. He says, "Trees were felled, junked and piled near the roadway and loaded onto the sleigh in roughly eight foot lengths". As he points out, it took a lot of sleigh loads for a winter's supply.

It is hoped that these few recollections will do honor to the farmers' helpers. . . their faithful horses.

[Published in *The Recaller*, May 1996.]

---

"Farm labor followed the regular cycles of nature: cultivating, planting, husbanding and harvesting in general. Much of it was of the back-breaking type and one was greatly relieved when each of these tasks was completed. The pace was slow as nature took its course, teaching many lessons to those who would listen and observe. Sunrise and sunset, the phases of the moon, the four seasons, the starry skies, the wind and rain all pointed to the hand of a wise creator providing for his people who over the centuries have observed and been guided by these same elements. On a farm the worker saw, touched and breathed these generous gifts of God."

- Father Arthur O'Shea, *It Happened in Iona.*

# A Well Story

In August of 1855, while William Ross of Flat River was away from home, his daughter went to their well to draw some cold water. The young girl was unable to get the bucket to sink into the water and when she noted that something was in the well, she ran to tell her mother.

The mother went to the well where her worst fears were realized, for there in the water – 25 feet below – was her three year old child. Nothing appeared above the surface of the water except the crown of her child's head.

Not knowing what was the best course to pursue, but well knowing that every moment was precious, the mother fastened the water bucket at the top of the well. She feared if the bucket were let down it would hit her little child's head below. She lowered the loop of the rope into the well, but it would only reach half way down, so she slid down the rope as far as it would permit and climbed the rest of the way down. After snatching her stiff unconscious child out of the water, the mother made a pouch by holding her long apron in her teeth. She placed her child in the pouch and began to climb back up. Bracing her back against the side of the well, the mother pushed on the opposite side of the well with her hands and wedged her toes into cracks in the stones. The climb was slow, but when she reached the end of the rope, she was able to pull her way to the top of the well.

But her child showed no signs whatever of returning animation; her limbs were cold and stiff and she had not the slightest pulsation over the region of the heart. Still, Mrs. Ross was resolved to do all that was possible to resuscitate her child and accordingly administered a remedy common in cases of exhaustion. She pried her child's mouth open with a spoon handle and poured in some whiskey. She then immersed the child in a hot bath. There were still no signs of life. She rubbed and chafed the little body with moist and hot wrappings and then bathed her again. A third hot bath was tried and while the mother must have been discouraged, she did not give up. Finally the child gasped for breath and then gave a faint cry. The child was swathed in flannel and put to bed. In a few hours, the child was awake and as happy as ever.

When William Ross came home that evening, he saw his little daughter was hale and hearty, where he might have seen a little corpse and the family disconsolate in tears.

This story has appeared in three issues of *The Recaller* and in several Island newspapers.

# Some Thoughts on Wells

*Hesta MacDonald*

It is easy to forget when we look at the green fields of Prince Edward Island that, when early settlers arrived, most of the land was covered with woods which had to be cleared. Clearing wooded areas, however, caused many small springs which had supplied the settlers with water to dry up. A good example is the small stream in Orwell where formerly three mill dams were supplied with water from springs which have now disappeared.

The change in natural water supplies made it necessary for farmers and other homeowners to dig wells rather than bring water from diminishing streams and springs. In later years, following the introduction of digging machines, people started replacing hand dug with machine dug wells.

One oft-related tale of the rescue of a child who had fallen into a well tells how William Ross's wife climbed down the well and snatched the inert little child from the water.

My husband's family credits their horse with averting the death of a child. The tale describes how a small child was peering down the well when their black horse grasped the child's clothing in its teeth and dragged the little one away from danger. The horse, as we can appreciate, won the family's deepest gratitude, and it lived out its life with every comfort the family could provide.

Sometimes in summer, a well dried up and had to be sunk deeper or had to be cleaned out. This could be hazardous because of the lack of oxygen at the bottom of the well. In Little Sands, a man named James MacDonald (known locally as Jimmie Taylor) lost his life from suffocation while cleaning the well on the property later owned by the late Peter Richards.

On a lighter note, a Flat River lady relates an experience from her childhood in Heatherdale. She was in the well house when a big rooster flew in and flapped right down into the well. She didn't know what to do, but instinctively she grabbed the bucket and let it down into the water. "And", she concludes, "when I pulled it up, up came the rooster, sitting on the bucket."

Viola Gillis tells of how her father, the late Eddie MacDonald, fell down a well on their property in Flat River. He was able to inch his way back up to ground level despite having rubber boots full of water, a broken pelvis and several other serious injuries.

Stories like this, and that of Mrs. Ross and her baby, indicate what we are capable of when faced with a life or death situation.

[Published in *The Recaller*, October 1995.]

# Gus Ross: Well Driller

*Hesta MacDonald*

"The pioneers settled as near a spring as they could", was the first comment of Gus Ross as he recalled his knowledge of wells and well digging in Belfast. His own house was hauled from its original location at the shore, its kitchen was removed and still serves as a woodshed and shop. A new kitchen was then added to the main part of the house, dating back to 1855. The move from the shore location was made possible by using a well rather than relying on a spring for water.

Mr. Ross's uncle, John Hughie Ross of Point Prim, was the local well digger from around 1900 until the 1920's, when he passed the equipment of the trade to Gus's cousin Frank, known locally as "Big Frank Ross".

Gus used to help his cousin digging wells. He recalls how a diviner would "witch" for water, using a forked willow branch which would turn downward when the diviner came to an underground stream.

An open well would be shoveled down to bedrock, and would be three or four feet in diameter. Gus remembers that digging a well "took a week or so. . . depending on the ground." The average depth of a well was 60 or 65 feet, although some were much deeper. Gus cited Allan Cameron's well in Caledonia as being 215 feet deep, making it one of the deepest wells in the area.

[Published in *The Recaller*, October 1995.]

**Gus Ross.**
[Photo courtesy of Marion MacRae.]

# Once an Issue Always an Issue

*Mary Ross*

In the early days, Northumberland Strait was a passageway to the mainland in the summer and a barrier in the winter. At times, the settlers were virtually prisoners. It is understandable, then, that from early times to the present day Island citizens have been clamoring for everything from canoes to causeways to connect them socially and economically with the rest of Canada.

The following is taken from a report by Thomas Appleton, Marine Historian, Department of Transport in the late 1800's.

According to the report, the first craft sent to the Island by Ottawa in an effort to keep winter communication open with the mainland, was the *Northern Light*. This boat was built in Quebec for $50,000. It was 144 feet in length and was designed for a speed of 14 knots.

The *Northern Light* arrived in Charlottetown on December 7, 1876, under the command of Captain A. Finlayson of Point Prim. The high hopes for a service between Pictou and Georgetown were quickly dashed when on her first trip, the steering gear failed at the entrance to Pictou harbour. Constant repairs were required, as this wooden ship was not built for ice conditions. Despite these troubles, service from Georgetown to Pictou continued at a cost of $13,000, while the purser took in $2,357.06 in passenger fares, freight, and mail charges.

In the winter of 1887-88, the *Northern Light* was badly damaged and was withdrawn from service. She was sold in 1890.

The people of Prince Edward Island protested vigorously that the promise of an efficient winter ferry service, which had been one of the conditions of confederation, had not been met.

The province brought the matter to the attention of the Imperial Parliament at Westminster, claiming compensation of five million dollars against the Canadian Government for breach of contract.

Britain referred the matter to Ottawa, without taking direct action, and the federal government appropriated a sum of $150,000 for the start of a new service to be maintained by up-to-date vessels.

The first of these was the *Stanley*. The *Stanley* made her first run from Charlottetown to Pictou on December 18, 1888. It was built in Scotland and was made of high tensile steel. She had triple expansion engines of 2,300 horsepower, the *Stanley* was a powerful ship and could steam at 15 knots.

The next ship to be put on the run from Georgetown to Pictou was the *Minto*. She had a straight stem, a cruiser stern, and she was fitted with steam machinery that indicated 2,900 horsepower. Capt. Angus Brown was in command of the *Stanley* and Capt. Allan Finlayson was in command of the *Minto*. Captain Finlayson was also master of Marine and Fisheries Service. Both men were from the Belfast district. By 1909, the traffic required a third ship, and the *Earl Grey* was added.

The *Earl Grey* was built by Vickers, Sons and Maxim at Barrows, England. She was designed by Charles Duguid, a naval architect at the Marine Department in Ottawa.

Captain Angus Brown was transferred from the *Stanley* and went to England with his crew to take over the *Earl Grey*. She was a powerful ship with triple expansion engines of 6,500 horsepower and a speed of 17 knots.

The *Earl Grey* was comfortable and attractively furnished. The public rooms were finished in mahogany, with white enameled deckheads, velvet plush upholstery, electric lights in brass, and cut glass mountings. She had an extra suite of rooms for distinguished official guests.

The *Earl Grey* was sold to Russia in 1914. She was used as an ice-breaker during the war and was scrapped in 1959. The wheel house is preserved in the Maritime Museum in Moscow. The *Minto* followed the *Earl Grey* to Russia in 1915 and is believed to have been wrecked off the Norwegian coast. In 1917, the *Prince Edward Island* went into service between Borden and Tormentine.

[Published in *The Recaller*, November 1989.]

---

*Jessie Nicholson MacKinnon:*

**Universal Cathedral Radio**

[Published in *The Recaller*, October 1994.]

In the early 1920's, when I was just a little girl, I remember my grandfather, John Nicholson, going to a community meeting in the old Flat River Hall to discuss the possibility of purchasing a radio for the district. Radio was a relatively new thing then, and not many understood how it worked. And I remember, after he got home from the meeting, asking my grandfather, "How does this radio thing work anyway?" "Well, it's like this", Grampa replied, "if they cut off a dog's tail in New York, we'd hear him barking here in Flat River".

I guess technology has come a long way since then.

# Remembering Changes in Transportation

*Hesta MacDonald*

This reflection goes back 53 years, to the day I came to Little Sands as a bride. Crossing Northumberland Strait on the first *Prince Nova* ferry was a different experience for a girl who grew up surrounded by farm lands and apple orchards. The *Prince Nova* carried a maximum of seventeen cars and she rode the waves like an empty washtub.

Arriving at the wharf in Wood Islands, I was struck by a picturesque scene unlike any I had seen heretofore. Probably typical of an Island fishing wharf of that time, there were piles of lobster traps, ropes, buoys and other accoutrements of the trade. Several boats were lying at anchor, for the fishermen had already brought in the day's catch. Shanties, where the families of the fishermen lived for the two months of the lobster fishing season, were beside the road near the wharf.

Over the ensuing decades, I made the crossing from Wood Islands to Caribou dozens of times, on a succession of ferry boats, each larger and more comfortable than those that had gone before.

Trains in Prince Edward Island are but a memory now, but they provided an enjoyable, relaxing way to travel, as well as transporting goods to and from the Island. Of course, just as travel today may be disrupted by winter storms, there were times when train journeys were also delayed.

Today's children will never know the excitement of watching a train rumbling and puffing into a station. Nor will they know the contented feeling of being wakened at night by the whistle of a train approaching a crossing. Even the rails have been torn up and replaced by walking trails.

Gradually, the narrow red roads of the Island had been widened, built up, ditched, and most have been paved. When we lived in Eldon in the 1950's, the Trans Canada Highway from Wood Islands to Charlottetown was being constructed.

It would seem, nevertheless, that progress often demands a stern sacrifice. In my early years on Prince Edward Island, every drive to Charlottetown gave an opportunity to admire the beautiful row of birch trees along the roadside in Cherry Valley. And then in one day, all those trees were torn out in order to widen the road for the Trans Canada Highway. Travel was made more rapid, but something of rare beauty was lost forever.

Some thirty years ago it seemed as if a bridge-causeway-tunnel would be constructed to link P.E.I. with New Brunswick. The approaches were actually built, but the project was shelved, and not until 1997 when Confederation Bridge was opened, did the "Fixed Link" become a reality.

In 53 brief years, horse-drawn traffic has disappeared, trains have gone, and the Borden ferry has lapsed into history.

[Published in *The Recaller*, April 1999.]

---

# The Wood Islands Ferry
*Dr. Stewart MacDonald*

During the start of the 20th century, Wood Islands was a very prosperous farming area with numerous cattle, sheep, horses and hens. Then there was a popular move to build a longer and bigger wharf for the shipping of farm products and a place for fishing boats. As the wharf grew longer, the more sand crept in from the east and choked out the use of the wharf. They kept lengthening it until it went beyond the main shore to the center end of the island where the lighthouse now stands. Yet, the only way to get to the Island was around by the road that goes down to the shore where stood the old grist mill, saw mill, and before that a carding mill to the west of the road.

There was bold water[1] at Little Sands wharf and it was closer to Pictou Landing than Wood Islands, but politics played a part and it was decided to make a harbour by cutting a waterway between the two islands through a large area of sand and dredging the mud, clay, and sand which was between the islands and the mainland, and placing the fill to make the roadway which joins the lighthouse island to the mainland. This is where the tides come into the so-called harbor from the east.

Although the surrounding sand causes considerable trouble due to wind drift, storms, and currents, frequent dredging overcame the problems. Another problem is that the steel sheeting to hold back the sand between the two islands keeps rusting and eroding.

The ferry was a good thing for the eastern end of the Island as well as for Wood Islands.

[Published in *The Recaller*, June 1998.]

[1] The term "bold water" is described in the dictionary as "abrupt or steep, as a cliff".

# Electricity – Don't Take it for Granted

*Hesta MacDonald*

Today, we take electricity so much for granted that we seldom take time to recall those days of dependence on candles, lamps, and lanterns. Yet, most people who grew up in Belfast, or in other parts of rural Prince Edward Island prior to the 1950's, can appreciate the many, many ways that electricity saves us work and enhances our lives.

Electricity had been extended from Charlottetown to Montague before the Second World War, but little, if anything, was done to further electrification for the duration of the war. In 1946, Dr. Harold Stewart began his medical practice in Eldon. Having grown up in Charlottetown, Dr. Stewart was well aware of the advantages of electricity, and of the hardships attendant on having to do without it. It was not only the convenience of electrical lighting, running water, and household equipment, but for the physician, electricity brought easier and more efficient means of sterilizing equipment. Dr. Stewart had installed a generator for domestic use, but while it could provide lights, it lacked power to run appliances.

 Dr. Stewart spearheaded a drive to persuade the Public Utilities Commission to bring electrical power to Eldon. The Commission was less than enthusiastic over such a project. By this time, electrical power came as far as Vernon Bridge, but the requisite number of subscribers (6 or 8 per mile) between Mt. Vernon and Eldon was lacking – hence no line would be put in there.

The alternative was to bring the electric line through Kinross, Grandview, Lower Newtown, and hence to Eldon. The committee visited every household along that route in an effort to get enough subscribers. Dr. Stewart recalls that some were totally negative, while many were reluctant to spend the money to have their household wired. These objections he found to be well-founded. Many houses were at some distance from the road, incomes were small, and some people simply could not understand the improvements that electricity would bring to houses and barns. Finally, after two or three years, enough subscribers had signed up, and electricity came to Eldon in January of 1952.

Not every family subscribed to electricity in those first years. For some, the cost of wiring houses and barns, the dread of the monthly electric bill, and doubts about the need of such a luxury, kept them from subscribing to it. In 1956, Dr. David MacKenzie, then residing in Eldon, offered to pay to have the local school wired. Far from being enthusiastic over that generous offer, many ratepayers were negative to the prospect, citing the cost of a monthly bill. Dr. MacKenzie's offer was accepted, however, and the Women's Institute paid the first month's bill.

Electric lights, running water, the efficiency and ease of heating our homes are the obvious first benefit of domestic electricity. In 1953, the Belfast Home Association installed an oil burner in the furnace of the doctor's residence. No more trips to the basement, no fire to keep stoked, and no ashes to remove!

Once the electricity was available, household appliances soon followed. One entrepreneur, quick to realize a potential market, had stocked up on major appliances in readiness for sales. One of the first purchases was the refrigerator, and another was the washing machine.

What a boon to farmers! Water pumped into the barns, milking machines, not to mention the barns and outbuildings, flooded with light with the flick of a switch! No more need to do the evening chores by dim lantern light.

Another aspect of rural life that underwent a major change when electricity came into the homes was that of entertainment. Television was installed in many homes by the mid-fifties, and almost every family had radio. These innovations certainly changed the cultural and social life of the family and the community, whether for better or worse is still a matter for debate.

[Published in *The Recaller*, April 1998.]

---

*Mary Nicholson Ross:*

Bill MacQueen, who was quite progressive, was one of the first in the area to have a tractor. He had it in the barn for several years before he decided to use it to do his fall ploughing. He hired a local man to drive the

tractor, and Bill was dispatched to Compton's with a can to get gas. It seemed he was no sooner back when he had to go again for another can of gas. On the way, he met his neighbor, Sid Stewart, to whom MacQueen admitted with a wry grin, "I'm either going to have to get a bigger can or a faster horse."

[Published in *The Recaller*, October 1994.]

# Chapter Nine

❧❧

# People

"The Belfast people are in the habit of making history, as well as remembering it."

*- The Guardian*, 1 August 1953.

**Sir Andrew MacPhail, 1924.**
[Prince Edward Island Public Archives and Records Office, Accession 2320, Item 2-12.]

# Belfasters in *Past and Present of P. E. I.*

Published in 1907, *Past and Present of Prince Edward Island*, edited by Hon. D. A. MacKinnon and Hon. A. B. Warburton, contained brief biographies of Island men. Over the past twenty-five years, many profiles of Belfast residents which appeared in *Past and Present* were reprinted in *The Recaller* newsletter. Following are some of these profiles.

## Donald Docherty

Capt. Donald Docherty, late of Cardigan Bridge, Lot 53, Kings County, died on February 29, 1904 at the ripe old age of 84 years, and was born in Belfast in 1821. In his youth he served as pilot and captain in the coasting trade and in about 1861, in association with his brothers-in-law Richard, George and Francis Panting, and his brother, Angus, he engaged in ship-building at Pinette and Red Point.

Capt. Docherty was a son of Angus and Catherine (McLeod) Docherty, the former of whom was born in Portree, Scotland, and at the age of 9 years came to P.E.I. on the ship *Polly*, accompanying his parents, Donald and Ann (Stewart) Docherty. Catherine McLeod was also a native of Portree, Scotland and descended from Lord McLeod of Portree. She was a daughter of Malcolm and Effie (McDonald) McLeod, the latter being of the Glengarry McDonalds. Two of her brothers were officers in the British army in the Battle of Waterloo, receiving honorable mention by the Duke of Wellington. One of them, Lieut. William McLeod, receiving medals. The latter came to P.E.I. and settled at Orwell.

Ann Stewart's grandfather was a cousin of Prince Charley and concealed him for 3 months at his house in the Highlands, this traitor being brought to the new world by Angus Docherty. The latter had two brothers, Findlay and Donald, who lived at Seal River. Capt. Donald Docherty had two brothers, Malcolm and Angus, of Belfast.

Capt. Docherty married Jennie Panting, daughter of Francis and Jennie (Fraser) Panting. Francis Panting was born in Oxford, England, and was a son of William and Ann (Pope) Panting, while his wife was born in Inverness, Scotland, and was a daughter of Angus and Jennie (Shaw) Fraser. Rev. Donald Fraser, the noted minister, of London, England, was a relative as was Rev. Allan Fraser of Belfast.

To Capt. Donald and Jennie Docherty were born the following children: Effie, wife of William McKenzie, of Cable Head; Mary A., wife of Enoch Paige, merchant of Boston, Massachusetts; Jennie P., wife of Angus Sutherland of Cardigan Bridge; Laura A., wife of Arthur E. Guild, of Boston, Massachusetts and Vermont; Alice M., wife of George Goff;

Katie, at home; Richard, deceased; Donald, a farmer in Lot 53, Kings County; William, at home; Angus, deceased; George, who owns and operates the old homestead in Lot 53; John Malcolm, of Cardigan, an artist; Annie, wife of Charles McEachern, of Belfast.

[Published in *The Recaller*, June 1986.]

# W. J. Emery

W. J. Emery, an enterprising merchant and successful farmer in Lot 62, Queens County, was born at Wood Islands, July 17, 1859, and is the son of John and Margaret Hume Emery.

The paternal grandfather, Peter Emery, was a native of Perth, Scotland, and came to P.E.I. in 1801, settling near Georgetown, moving shortly afterwards to Wood Islands, where he lived until his death, in 1879. He was the father of seven children: James, Peter, John, Ann, Mary, William, and Robert.

To the subjects parents were born five children: Catherine, wife of William Young, a farmer; Peter, now deceased, who married Miss McPherson; John W., and two that died in infancy. John Emery owned a farm at Wood Islands, Cross Roads, which he successful operated until the time of his death in 1861. In politics, he supported the Liberal Party, and his religious affiliation was with the Presbyterian Church.

W. J. Emery received a good district school education. He has 25 acres of land under the plow and on this he has resided since 1886, having formerly lived at Wood Islands, where he carried on shipbuilding and carpentry.

On October 26, 1881, Mr. Emery married Isabella McRae, daughter of John and Christina McRae, and to them have been born four children: Agnes, educated at Prince of Wales College and now teaching school; Cora and Jonetta, at home; and Peter J., who assists in the operation of the family farm. Mr. Emery is politically a Liberal, fraternally an Orangeman, and a member of the Presbyterian Church, of which he is a trustee.

[Submitted by Peggy Gauthier. Published in *The Recaller*, November 2000.]

# Frank Halliday

Frank Halliday, who owns and operates a fine farm on Lot 57, was a native son of P.E.I. and was born at Charlottetown. His father Capt. John Halliday, was born on the same farm on which the subject now resides, and at the age of 13 years he went to sea. He owned a number of vessels and served as Master of many others, and in later life confined his operations mainly to the coast trade. Subsequently, he went to British

Columbia and engaged in the lumbering business, owning a slope on the river. He was killed there, at the age of 57 years by a falling tree.

The paternal grandfather, James E. Halliday, lived on the same farm now owned by the subject and engaged extensively in shipbuilding, being himself a master shipwright, and building many vessels for Benjamin Davis and others.

The paternal great-grandfather, Thomas Halliday, was a native of Edinburgh, Scotland and in 1806 came to Pictou, Nova Scotia. He was a successful architect and builder and built a stone house at Pictou before coming to Belfast. Upon coming here, he took up the land on which the subject now resides and here engaged in farming. He was a highly educated man, having studied in the schools and colleges of Edinburgh. He married a Miss Hague, of Edinburgh.

The subjects paternal grandmother bore the maiden name of Belle MacDonald, her family having come to P.E.I. on the ship *Rambler* in 1806. The subject's mother, whose maiden name was Annie Rowan, was a native of Ayr, Ayrshire, Scotland, where she married Mr. Halliday. She is now living with her son on the homestead.

To Capt. John and Annie Halliday were born the following children: Frank; Minnie, wife of Charles Horn, of Boston, Massachusetts; Annie, of Boston; Albert and William of Boston; John, deceased; Artemas who at the age of 22 years, was killed by an accident in a gold mine in Colorado; Maude; James, of Boston; Angus, of Boston; and Fred who is in the Northwest Territory. The subject's farm was, in 1903, the scene of a most interesting event, it being the 100th anniversary celebration of the arrival of the ship *Polly* at Belfast.

The subject of this sketch received a good district school education and was reared to the life of a farmer.

[Submitted by Peggy Gauthier. Published in *The Recaller*, April 2001.]

## Malcolm McLean

Malcolm McLean, a progressive and successful agriculturist at Little Sands, was born at this place on November 20, 1855, and is the son of Angus and Mary (Blue) McLean, both of whom were natives of Scotland and who were farming people all their lives.

The paternal grandparents Laughlin and Ann (MacEachern) McLean, who were also both natives of Scotland, came to P.E.I. in an early day and here died.

Malcolm McLean attended the district schools in his neighbourhood and was reared to the life of a farmer. Subsequently, however, he served an apprenticeship at the trade of stone cutting and followed that occupation about 28 years, during which time he was a partner in the monumental firm of Cairns & McLean at Charlottetown. In 1897, Mr. McLean retired from this business and came to his present farmstead to which he has since devoted his attention. The place comprises 80 acres of well improved land and in addition Mr. McLean also owns 93 acres in Queens County.

On September 19, 1892, Mr. McLean married Annie Younker, a daughter of Lemuel and Mary Ann (Offer) Younker, the former a native of North River, the latter of Charlottetown, the father dying on May 6, 1888 and the mother yet living. To Mr. and Mrs. McLean have been born six children: Mary E., deceased; Harold; Helen; Lemuel M.; Victoria; and James E.

[Submitted by Peggy Gauthier. Published in *The Recaller*, September 2001.]

## John R. McRae

John R. McRae, a successful farmer and miller at Roseberry, Lot 60, where he was born on April 16, 1865. He is a son of James and Sarah (Campbell) McRae. The father, a native of Ponds, born in 1822, and the mother, of Pinette, born in 1830. Her father, Alexander Campbell, a farmer, was a native of Rosshire, Scotland and came to P.E.I. on the *Polly* in 1803.

The paternal grandfather, Donald McRae, was a native of Scotland and came to P.E.I. in 1803 on the ship *Polly*, settling at Ponds, where he followed farming throughout his active years.

James McRae followed a seafaring life for over 20 years, rising to the rank of captain. He was the father of five children namely: Kate, deceased; Jeanette, wife of Fred Whittle, an upholster in Boston, Massachusetts, now deceased; Kenneth met his death by drowning; John R. is the next in birth; Richard C., a farmer residing near the subject and a member of the firm of McRae Brothers. James McRae was a Liberal in politics, and a Presbyterian in religious faith.

John R. McRae received a good district school education and was reared to the life of a farmer. This he has followed during his mature years, and in connection with it he operates a sawmill established by his father. He also does much contracting and carpenter work, in which he has been very successful. He owns 150 acres of land.

In 1895 Mr. McRae married Jeanette Martin, daughter of Donald Martin, of Belle River. He is a trustee of St. John's Church, and fraternally he is a member of St. Andrew's Lodge Ancient Free and Accepted Masons, at Montague Bridge.

[Submitted by Peggy Gauthier. Published in *The Recaller*, October 2000.]

# John Nicholson

John Nicholson who operates a farm in Lot 60, Queens County, was born in Flat River on May 24, 1848, and is the son of John and Catherine (Bell) Nicholson, the father a farmer born at Belle Creek.

The paternal grandfather, Alex Nicholson was born in Scotland on the Isle of Skye and was a passenger on the ship *Polly* in 1803, settling in Belle Creek. He was a successful farmer and died in 1820. He married Miss Mary Nicholson, and to them were born the following children: Neil, who died in 1888; Isabella, who died in 1841; John, the subjects father, who died in 1858; Samuel, who died in 1866 in Australia; Alexina, who died in 1883.

To John and Catherine Nicholson were born the following children: Isabella, the widow of Hector Morrison, deceased; John, the subject of this sketch; Alex, deceased; Samuel; Catherine, deceased, wife of Ronald McPhee of Little Sands, Kings County, farmer; Mary, wife of William Boyd, a merchant and rancher in British Columbia.

The subject secured a good education in district schools and has followed throughout his life the vocation of farming. He is the owner of 185 acres of fine land. Mr. Nicholson had lived on his parents place all his life. In politics, he is a conservative and in religion, a Presbyterian.

In 1882, Mr. Nicholson was united in marriage to Jeanette Campbell, a daughter of Donald and Flora (Gillis) Campbell, the former a native of Applecross, Scotland and the latter of the Isle of Skye. To Mr. and Mrs. Campbell were born the following children: Jessie, the subjects wife; Flora; John; and Mary M.

To Mr. and Mrs. Nicholson have been born three children, namely: John, engaged with the Gold Roof Mining Company at Butte, Montana; Donald C., at home; and Alex N., at home.

[Published in *The Recaller*, October 1986 and October 2001.]

# Magnus Ross

Magnus Ross, a substantial citizen and successful agriculturist of Lot 60, Queens County, was born at Flat River on September 13, 1861, and is a son of John H. and Elizabeth (McDonald) Ross, the former of whom was born on the place where the subject now resides on May 7, 1833, and died in 1886. His wife was born at Little Sand[s], on September 25, 1833, and died in 1884. They were the parents of nine children, namely: Ewen, deceased; Magnus, subject of this sketch; John H., a farmer at Point Prim; Sarah C. in Massachusetts; Donald J., a farmer at Flat River; Hector, who resides with the subject; Francis, deceased; Alex, a carpenter at Flat River; Florence, who resides in California.

The paternal great-great grandfather, Ewen Ross, was a native of Scotland, but never left his native land. His widow came to P.E.I. in the ship *Polly*, in 1803, and died shortly afterwards. Their son, John Ross, the subject's great-grandfather, was a native of the Isle of Skye, Scotland, and accompanied his mother to P.E.I. in 1803, settling at Flat River, Lot 60, where the subject of this sketch now resides. He married Miss Mary Nicholson on board the ship *Polly*. He died in 1813.

Their son, Ewen Ross, grandfather of the subject, was born at Flat River in 1807, and died in 1861. He married Fanny Macdonald in 1831. She was born on the Isle of Skye, Scotland, in 1793, and came to P.E.I. August 5, 1830. She died in 1871.

The subject's maternal grandfather, Magnus McDonald, was a native of the Isle of Mull, Scotland, and came here as one of a party aboard a survey ship and himself helped to survey part of the Maritime Provinces.

**Magnus Ross with his granddaughter Frances Ross, ca. 1945** [Photo courtesy of Marion MacRae.]

The subject was reared under the paternal roof and secured a practical education in the district schools. He has followed farming throughout his life, owning 130 acres of land. He gives especial attention to dairying, sending the dairy products to the cheese factory at Belle River. Mr. Ross is independent in his political attitude, preferring to vote for the men and measures that most nearly harmonize with his own views. For some time he has served as director of schools. In religion he is a member of the Presbyterian church.

In 1900 Mr. Ross married Sarah Stewart, a daughter of John and Mary (McKenzie) Stewart, the father a native of Belle River, and to this union have been born two children: Stewart J. (born 1902) and Augustus F. (born 1904).

[Published in *The Recaller*, November 1986.]

---

# We Remember Bertha Longard West
## 1868-1963
*Helen West MacDonald*

Born in St. Margaret's Bay, Nova Scotia, on October 27, 1868, Bertha Longard was the eldest of five children born to Robert Longard and his wife Catherine Boutilier. A cobbler by trade, Mr. Longard moved his family to Eldon in the early 1880's. Except for brief visits with relatives in Boston, Toronto, or points in the Maritimes, Bertha Longard, our "Gammy" spent most of her life in Eldon.

In 1894, Gammy married Thomas Frederick West, a teacher at Eldon School. They lived briefly in a house on the Wharf Road. It was here that their first children, Martin Cedric and Blanche Hypatia were born.

During the years 1897-1899, the family lived in eastern Nova Scotia, where my grandfather (who had been ordained in 1897) served in various charges of the Anglican church. Their youngest child (my father), Roberts Sinclair was born in Ship Harbour in 1899. The following year, a call to serve at St. Peter's Cathedral in Charlottetown brought the family back to the Island. That fall, while on a trip to Boston, my grandfather became ill and died suddenly on October 20, 1900. With three young children aged 3½, 2½, and 10 months, Gammy found herself head of a one-parent family.

In 1903, Gammy's younger sister, Ida May Lantz, died leaving three young daughters. After a few years, ill health forced their father to move to California. The "Lantz girls" as we came to know them, moved from Boston in 1907 to live with their Aunt Bertha's family in Eldon. Gertrude was 7, Josephine 9, and Grace 11. Their ages corresponded with Gammy's own children, and they all shared happy memories of growing up together. In later years, Josephine wrote, "Coming from living in a hotel with a maiden aunt and coming to P.E.I. was like heaven to us. We were all starving for love and received more than our share."

In 1937, after the death of my mother Emily Millar West, Gammy at age 69 again took on the task of motherhood. With five children ranging in age from 11 months to 10 years, this was no small responsibility. She had been living with my parents at the time and from then on, with her usual cheerful and humorous nature, spent many of her senior years nurturing us and encouraging us to become responsible adults.

One way in which she helped us forget our loss was with her love of music. Although she had no formal voice training, she enjoyed singing and teaching children to sing. She often organized community concerts and sang solos at these and in church choirs.

She also liked to create pretty things and hooked mats were her specialty. We had lots of fun watching or helping her make the patterns, stamp the canvas, and then dye the rags for the final product. She often stamped mats for others and carefully worked to get the patterns and colors just to her liking.

Another fun experience for us, especially my sisters and I, was Gammy's interest in millinery. With a new dent here and a re-arranged corsage or clump of feathers there or perhaps a fresh ribbon, she had a change of hats for each season.

Gammy's great love of reading no doubt helped develop her exceptional command of the English language. We grew to appreciate the written and spoken word.

I would be very remiss in not mentioning the extended family and many kind friends who helped and encouraged us at that time. None of us will ever forget the birthday cake and home-made ice cream that came yearly for each one from a very dear neighbor, or the beloved aunt who came so often to help out. But, to our dear Gammy who gave so much of herself in her loving care we are all very indebted.

In my memory she was like a cheery robin, for in addition to being round, she was bright and sort of chirpy. But most of all, she was bird-like in possessing a beautiful singing voice, sweet, true, and bell-like. Her manner showed refinement and graciousness. She had the ability to tell a story well, often with a laugh at herself.

**"Gammy" Bertha Longard West in 1956 at 88 years old.** [Photo courtesy of Bertie Cook.]

[Published in *The Recaller*, May 1997.]

---

"Women from Belfast proved by brilliant scholarship and later by professional skill, that they could engage in intellectual pursuits of equality with men."

- Malcolm MacQueen, *Hebridean Pioneers*.

# In Grandma's Day

*Joan Rooney*

In Grandma's day in Iona, it was quite a different age to live in. When I tell my children about it today, they look at me and say, "Now Mom, are you telling me it really was that way?" I tell them, "Yes, my dears, it was that way and we were very, very happy, although poor in material things, we had a wealth of peace and happiness." Grandma was a very busy woman then because she had to make do with so many things.

The house was of the old farm style with a large kitchen containing a big wooden table, wooden chairs and a wooden bench, for there were large families in those days. There was a large wood range stove with a tank on the end for water and an oven to do the baking. Of course, there was no such thing as buying bread. The wheat was taken to the mill and ground into flour, and Grandma used it to bake her bread.

There was a wood stove in the hall of the house to keep the family warm in the winter. Grandma would heat some sticks of wood and bricks to put in the beds to warm them up at night. She made heavy quilts to keep them warm. In the morning, the fire would have been burned out, so you can imagine how cold it was.

When Grandma had her babies, they were all born at home. There was a country doctor who was engaged a short while before the baby was due and a woman who lived in the district who would be called upon to help the doctor and stay with the mother until she was up and about. I guess the only time Grandma got a rest.

Along with all the housework, Grandma did many other things. She helped Grandpa with the outside work, as he had to walk behind all the machinery – there were no tractors then. She planted potatoes, hoed turnips and the vegetable garden, milked the cows and fed the calves.

It was Grandma's job to look after a large number of hens, and gather and clean the eggs, as they were taken to the store to trade for groceries. It was her job to kill a hen when it was needed for a pot of soup or to be roasted in the oven. She had to pluck the hen or chicken, and clean it well. Oh, how the family enjoyed the chicken or the big pot of soup!

Grandma had to wash the clothes in the big round tub with an old fashioned washboard. There was no electricity, so the water had to be pumped (if you were fortunate enough to have a pump). If not, and if you had a stream of water on your farm, you would have to carry the water in buckets up the hill, as there always were hills. She would heat the water in a big pot called a boiler, and then pour the hot water into a tub. Grandma made her own soap, and she would have to rub the clothes on the washboard to get them clean. She usually soaked, washed, rinsed and sometimes boiled the clothes in bluing to make them white. Sometimes she would hang them on the line, or in summer she would spread the sheets and white things on the grass or shrubs. There were no dryers, so in winter she had to spread them around the house to dry. Imagine now with the pampers! Grandma had cloth diapers which had to be washed and dried continually.

Then, Grandma had to bake the bread and cook the meals. She made pickles, jams and jelly, and she salted or cured the meat. There were no refrigerators. Some families had ice houses – grandpa would cut ice in big squares from a fresh water pond, take them home and place them in the ice house and cover them with sawdust. If you didn't have an ice house, you would pump cold water in a tub and keep it in the cool basement under your house, or if there was a spring down at the stream, you would place it there to keep it cool. Grandma had to make the butter, and even with all her chores, she had to take care of the babies and little ones. Sometimes Grandma would be up all night when the little ones were sick. She never seemed to get sick herself.

With all that work, she always found time to knit, sew, make quilts and even hook mats and found time to do some fancy work, visit a sick person, cheer a friend who was sad, and help out in many ways. She also found time to go to a card game or a local dance in a house, time for her prayers, teaching the little ones, and attending church.

One tradition Grandma had, as there were not so many cakes and cookies baked before Christmas, was making dark fruit cake. It was made once a year and only served a small piece once in awhile. After Christmas, Grandma and maybe some of the children, would visit all the neighbors around to sample each others cakes.

Grandma was a busy woman who always had time for someone else – God Bless Grandma and also Grandpa!

[Published in *The Recaller*, June 1997.]

---

"The women of Belfast have always been eager for education. By 1900, when women physicians were rare everywhere, Belfast had seven of her daughters to that noble calling. They were: Annie Campbell MacRae of Pinette Ponds; Annie D. MacRae of Flat River; Anne Young of Pinette; Florence MacRae of Pinette Ponds; Florence MacDonald of Pinette; Eliza Margaret MacKenzie of Flat River; and Isabella MacPhail of Orwell."

- Malcolm MacQueen, speaking at the 150th Anniversary Celebrating the Arrival of the Selkirk Settlers, August 6, 1953.

# We Remember Edythe VanIderstine
## 1896-1989
*Hesta MacDonald*

The Belfast District was deeply enriched when, following the cessation of the hostilities of the Great War of 1914-18, Justin VanIderstine brought his British "War Bride" home to P.E.I.

Edythe VanIderstine, whose maiden name was Baldock, was born in the resort town of Eastbourne, England, in 1896. As a young girl she attended singing school and resided with her mother who was deaf.

Edythe and Justin were married in England and came to Canada in 1919. Although she never talked about the horrors or privation of wartime, saying only she "just wanted to forget", she vividly recalled the seasickness that was with her all the way on the two week crossing of the Atlantic.

For a time the young couple lived in Vernon River with Justin's parents, before taking up their lifelong residence in Eldon. It was in Eldon that they brought up their family of three sons and two daughters.

Life in Prince Edward Island must have had many days of loneliness for Mrs. Van (as she was affectionately known in the community). She did make trips back to her hometown, but her parents had passed away.

**Edythe and Justin VanIderstine.** [Photo courtesy of Peggy and Billy Penny.]

[Published in *The Recaller*, May 1995.]

Edythe VanIderstine made a significant contribution to the community in a number of ways. For years she was a faithful choir member of St. John's Presbyterian Church, and a life member of the Ladies Auxiliary. She was a loyal member of the Eldon Women's Institute. As the director of the plays the Institute staged from time to time, Mrs. Van brought a very serious mien, which never quite hid the twinkle in her eye.

Edythe Van Iderstine died in 1989. In paying tribute to Mrs. Edythe VanIderstine, we recall she possessed a gracious good humour and a gentle wit, and that she exemplified good citizenship in her adopted land.

# We Remember Christine Matheson Ross
## 1893 – 1978
*Mary Ross*

Christine Ann Matheson was born in Belle River on July 13, 1893 to Allan and Mary (Murchison) Matheson.

When Christine was 16 years old, she went to Cambridge, Massachusetts to live with her sister Annie and her husband James MacDonald of Cape Breton. Later Christine was accepted at Chester Hospital, where she received training as a Registered Nurse. Following graduation, she enlisted with a Harvard Unit of Boston and went overseas as a nursing sister. In England, she transferred to a Canadian company and spent the remaining war years in field hospitals in France.

By most people, the number thirteen is considered unlucky, but Christine didn't feel that way. She was born on July 13th and from that time number thirteen crept into many things in her life. She had related that there were thirteen ships in the convoy going overseas, and thirteen days crossing the ocean. The convoy landed in England on the 13th day of the month and to follow through, she went to France on the 13th.

Christine survived World War I and returned to PEI to nurse her mother who was ill. In 1920, she married William Ross, and together they brought up their six children in North Pinette; Alexander, Elliott and Mary (Mrs. Donald Morrison) both deceased, Elinor (Mrs. Donald MacPherson) of Charlottetown, Ann Bruck of Florida, and Peggy Criss of Kamloops, BC. The number thirteen creeps in again in the lives of Christine's family. Elinor's three children were born on the 13th of the month; Christine's daughter Ann was born on December 13th; Elliott's daughter was born on February 13th; Elliott's grandson was born on March 13th; and a great-grandson was born on May 13th.

**Christine Matheson Ross.** [Photo courtesy of Donna Knox.]

Christine received great praise from Dr. Brehaut of Murray River. She was the nurse attending when he did surgery on a patient in her own home with the kitchen table substituting for an operating table. After this successful operation, the doctor was heard saying, "If I had a nurse like Christine Ross, we could run our own hospital."

Christine Matheson Ross died on November 16, 1978. She is fondly remembered and highly respected. Her contribution to the war effort and her work in the community as a nurse attending (sometimes by herself) the birth of many Belfasters is something for which we can all be proud.

[Published in *The Recaller*, September 1994.]

# Sir Andrew MacPhail
## 1864-1938

The MacPhail house was the boyhood home of Sir Andrew MacPhail who, in his time, was well-known both nationally and internationally. He graduated in medicine from McGill University in Montreal and remained there on the faculty for thirty years. However, his outstanding work was in the literary field as a social critic, lecturer, author and editor, and it was for his accomplishments in this area that he was knighted in 1918. Out of his vast amount of writings, *The Master's Wife* is considered his best work, partly for the way it shows his rare skill with words but, too, because it shows how he appreciated and approved of the way of life of his parents' day. The setting of the book was in Orwell and the main characters were his parents – the Master was MacPhail's father, a school master and inspector, and the Master's wife was MacPhail's mother, the mother of a family of ten. The story depicts the traditional lifestyle of a Scottish Canadian family on a small Prince Edward Island farm in the late 1800's. MacPhail was considered one of Canada's best known social critics and all through this book we see how he uses this gift to express his warm feelings about the culture, beliefs, values, and pleasures of life in his parents home in Orwell.

*The Master's Wife* is a special book and a valuable social history of this community in the 1800's. Although MacPhail's many faceted life was spent mainly in Montreal along with service in World War I, he found time to spend his summers in Orwell where lay his loyalty to its people and their way of life.

[Published in *The Recaller*, December 1988.]

# Chapter Ten

❧

# Celebrations and Recreation

"You in Belfast have much to be proud of. Do not let the spirit of our forefathers pass from you. Let this anniversary be a living memory to those who are here today. Pass on the pride of this occasion to your children so that they, on the two hundredth anniversary, may point with satisfaction to your efforts. And so also on the three hundredth or even the five hundredth anniversary, the people who celebrate here can look with joy and pride on a heritage well preserved and handed down to them."

- Premier A. W. Matheson, speaking at the 150th Anniversary Celebrating the Arrival of the Selkirk Settlers, August 4, 1953.

**The 100th Anniversary Celebrating the Arrival of the Selkirk Settlers (1903).**
**The ceremonies were held at Frank Halliday's field in Eldon.**
[Prince Edward Island Public Archives and Records Office, Accession 3423, Item 1.]

# 100<sup>th</sup> Anniversary Celebration

*Mary Ross and Viola Gillis*

"Belfast Honors 'The Polly Men'" was the news headline of *The Morning Guardian* on August 12, 1903.

It was fitting, then, that the Scotchmen of Belfast, descendants of the men of the *Polly* and their friends should celebrate the centennial of that eventful day in the history of our province. It was proper, too, that Sons of Scotland should join together to do honors to their forefathers and fan the fire of patriotism which makes the Scotchman respected the world over.

The day was an ideal one for such a gathering, and no more beautiful a site could have been selected. Far off to the north stretched the hills of Alexandra and Pownal, while to the east was Vernon River and Orwell capped with the giant spirals of beautiful churches. Nearer was the placid waters of Orwell Bay and a short distance to the west was the cove where the colonists first set foot on the portion of the new world which was to be their heritage.

All farm work was ceased for the time and everyone was imbued with the spirit characteristic of such an occasion. From Charlottetown, the ship, *City of London*, under the charge of Captain Craig, brought several hundred passengers. Some of Charlottetown's leading men arrived and hundreds came from the countryside for the 100<sup>th</sup> anniversary celebration.

The meeting place was about a mile from Eldon in Frank Halliday's field, at the head of Halliday's Wharf. Long before noon the carriages began to arrive and after dinner at two o'clock, the audience surrounded the platform and was listening attentively to the orators.

Rev. A. McLean Sinclair was chairman and among the guests were his Honor Lieutenant Governor McIntyre, Mrs. McIntyre, Premier Peters, Hon. D. A. McKinnon, Judge Hector C. McDonald, A. A. McLean, K. C. Martin, Alex Martin, with several of the older clansmen of the region.

The chairman in opening the proceedings stated the objective was to celebrate the arrival of the *Polly* and to raise money in connection with a monument to be erected. This famous vessel arrived on August 7<sup>th</sup>, 1803, followed on August 9<sup>th</sup> by the *Dykes*, and on August 29<sup>th</sup> by the *Oughton*.

Rev. Sinclair repeated his address in Gaelic. Alexander Matheson of Glen William and John Buchanan of Mount Buchanan then sang a Gaelic song entitled *Oban Emeric*, meaning the emigration song. The song had been composed by Mr. Buchanan's grandfather.

Judge MacDonald gave the first speech, on "The Coming of the Polly". He said most emigrants were from Skye, though some came from the interior of Invernesshire. Lord Selkirk arrived on the *Dykes*, several days after the *Polly*. He found the *Polly* colonists camping near the old French burial ground, which still remains. Among those arriving on the *Polly* was Dr. McAulay. Lord Selkirk gave him 1,102 acres of land.

Angus A. MacLean, spoke on "Life in the Woods". For a time, the early settlers lived in houses built of brush. Later, they built log houses with three rooms. The settlers first lived by fishing mackerel, herring, and cod which was plentiful in the Bay and the Pinette River. They made small clearings each year. They had troubles too, some years plagues of mice and grasshoppers destroyed their crops.

Alex Martin mentioned that we need the self-denial of our forefathers to maintain with dignity the heritage bestowed upon us.

A Gaelic song describing the country as the pioneers found it was given by Allan McMillan of Wood Islands, and Alexander Matheson of Lot 63. Later, a Gaelic song about the pioneers' treatment on the *Polly* was sung by Charles Morrison of Flat River, Daniel McMahon of Caledonia, and Allan McMillan of Wood Islands.

K. C. Martin gave praise to our forefathers for enduring the hardships and suffering to create a heritage for their children. With three cheers and singing, the meeting ended and the people began to return to their homes. The *City of London* sailed for Charlottetown at six and by sunset Belfast's most orderly and most memorable gathering was brought to a close.

[Published in *The Recaller*, Summer 1983.]

---

# 150th Anniversary Services
# at the Historic Belfast Church
*The Guardian*, August 3, 1953.

A week of celebration marking the 150th anniversary of the landing of the Selkirk Settlers at Belfast opened yesterday with a service at St. John's Presbyterian Church, conducted by the pastor, Rev. James E. Heathwood who came to the church in April of this year from Glasgow, Scotland.

A large congregation was present in the morning when Mr. Heathwood gave a stirring message based on the 124th Psalm. The speaker traced briefly the events leading up to the mass emigration of the Scottish Highlanders to America at the beginning of the 19th century.

He recalled after the defeat of the clansmen in the Jacobite rebellion, the land of the Scottish Chiefs was taken over by English landowners and since the Chief had no longer need for a band of fighting men, the clansman could not obtain the low rental rates to which he had been accustomed, with the result that life for him became unbearable. In some instances, open cruelty on the part of the landowner was resorted to.

None of the settlers who came to Belfast, he pointed out, were evicted tenants. They had previously intended to join their relatives in North Carolina, but on the advice of Lord Selkirk, they came to a British Colony instead.

The minister pointed out that whatever the reason for an emigrant's leaving, he will always consider Scotland his native land. Said Mr. Heathwood, "Our forefathers built this church and the church to them was the most important thing in their lives."

The evening service was conducted by the Rev. Wallace MacPherson, minister at Valleyfield United Church. He took for his text the 15th verse of the 2nd Philippians.

"The people who built this church", said Mr. MacPherson, "made it the center of their every activity. In so doing, they were shining as a light to the world. If we are to hold forth the word of life, we must re-discover and recognize God in our daily life."

The music for both services was under the direction of Mrs. M. W. MacDonald of Eldon. The choir was heard in two beautiful anthems, "Life Up Your Heads O Ye Gates", and "The Spacious Firmament On High".

[Published in *The Recaller*, July 1994.]

---

# Ice Racing

These notes are taken from the 1920 minutes of The Federal Driving Club:

"The first race was held on Pinette ice on January 1st. More than 500 people enjoyed the sport enough to attend despite the snow storm. Even the ladies waited to see the last heat.

A lack of advertising, unfortunately, caused the Newtown and Iona people to arrive too late to start their horses.

The presiding officer was E. L. Harrington, and the judges were W. D. MacKenzie and Ezra Larrabee. The timers were J. Buchanan and Ernest Manson."

"On February 28, 1920, a large crowd gathered to witness the best races ever on Pinette River ice. Horsemen included Neil Morrison, J. Robertson, D. N. Morrison, Percy MacLean, Willie Ross, and Austin MacMillan."

Racing continued as long as ice conditions remained good.

[Published in *The Recaller*, May 1996.]

# Trotters and Pacers

*Isabel MacDonald*

The history of horse racing dates back over many decades as the most popular sport and entertainment in the Belfast area. There have been a number of tracks in operation over the years. The current track at Pinette is the second track to operate in that community. The first track in Pinette was at the Pinette Ponds on property owned by the late Clarence MacKenzie, a great racing enthusiast and the proud owner of one of the great Pinette racers, the oddly named *WMX*. The Ponds track was in operation in the latter years of the 1950's and was eventually replaced by the present track in the early 1960's. The first starter and announcer was the late Tom McKenna from Village Green. Among other things, Tom was an auctioneer, and he used that skill to good advantage in calling the "heats" every summer Saturday afternoon at Pinette. (Races are now held on Wednesday evenings.) With Tom's death, the starter's microphone was passed to our own Donald MacKenzie, no stranger to the track as a driver of his own horse *Davey Harvester*. The faithful "timer" at the track was Cecil Moser, who never missed a race in the history of the track.

**A race at the Pinette Ponds Racetrack, 1960.**
[Photo courtesy of Viola Gillis. ]

Of course, the Pinette tracks were not the first tracks in the Belfast area. There was a very popular track in Garfield (behind the property currently owned by Darren and Sherry Hancock), in the early decades of the 1900's. Horses came by train to race from as far away as Summerside. Donald MacKenzie remembers his father, Willie Dan, racing his mare *Bellewood* at Garfield oval. He would likely find himself racing against some equally wily horsemen like Willie Ross from Garfield, Wilfred MacLean from Orwell Cove, and Neil Morrison from South Pinette with his pacer *Woodvale*.

In winter, ice racing took place at Gascoigne Cove and later, on the Pinette River. They raced a quarter mile on ice sleighs, riding sleighs or bikes. Some of the drivers at Gascoigne included: Malcolm Ross, Malcolm MacDonald, Lem Compton, Alex Campbell, Gus Ross, and Roddie MacKenzie.

**SCORE CARD**

**HORSE RACES AT GARFIELD**

ON

**PEOPLES' TRACK**

ON

**Wednesday, July 28th, 1920**

The Central Job Printery, 176 Kent St.,

**Cover of a 1920 Score Card from the Garfield Racetrack.**
[Courtesy of John M. MacKenzie.]

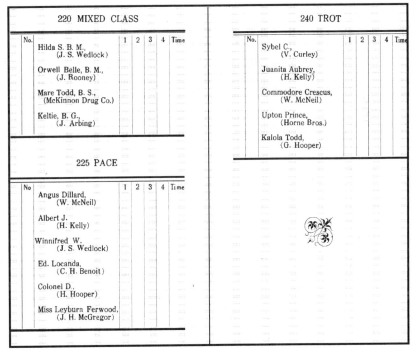

| 220 MIXED CLASS | | 1 | 2 | 3 | 4 | Time |
|---|---|---|---|---|---|---|
| Hilda S. B. M., (J. S. Wedlock) | | | | | | |
| Orwell Belle, B. M., (J. Rooney) | | | | | | |
| Mare Todd, B. S., (McKinnon Drug Co.) | | | | | | |
| Keltie, B. G., (J. Arbing) | | | | | | |

| 225 PACE | | 1 | 2 | 3 | 4 | Time |
|---|---|---|---|---|---|---|
| Angus Dillard, (W. McNeil) | | | | | | |
| Albert J. (H. Kelly) | | | | | | |
| Winnifred W. (J. S. Wedlock) | | | | | | |
| Ed. Locanda, (C. H. Benoit) | | | | | | |
| Colonel D., (H. Hooper) | | | | | | |
| Miss Leyburn Ferwood, (J. H. McGregor) | | | | | | |

| 240 TROT | | 1 | 2 | 3 | 4 | Time |
|---|---|---|---|---|---|---|
| Sybel C., (V. Curley) | | | | | | |
| Juanita Aubrey, (H. Kelly) | | | | | | |
| Commodore Crescus, (W. McNeil) | | | | | | |
| Upton Prince, (Horne Bros.) | | | | | | |
| Kalola Todd, (G. Hooper) | | | | | | |

**The line up for the July 28th race.** [Courtesy of John M. MacKenzie.]

[Published in *The Recaller*, May 1996.]

# The First Christmas in Our New Home

*Bertha Mae MacIntyre MacDonald*

The year of 1936 was drawing to it's close. The weather was cold, but not stormy and there was enough snow down for good travelling; we traveled by horse and sleigh, as we did not own a car.

We had been invited for Christmas dinner with my husband's family, as I was a new bride and not yet very experienced in the culinary arts. Our Christmas plans did not include much in the way of extras, but I had cleaned and polished the old house from top to bottom and we planned to have a tree, just a small one, for we had no store bought decorations.

On Christmas Eve, we went to the woods to cut and bring home our tree. It was a lovely green spruce, just the right size to stand on our living room table. I had never trimmed a tree before and my decorations had to be the result of my own ingenuity and imagination.

After I had set the tree in an old antique jar and placed it in the center of the table, I assembled my materials: cranberries, popcorn, tin foil, cotton wool, scissors, darning needle and a ball of fine red yarn. With the needle, I drew the yarn through berries one by one until I had a long red rope to twine around the tree. Next, I placed the popcorn and tiny balls of white cotton wool on the boughs to represent snow. I drew a star on a piece of cardboard and covered it with tin foil for the top of the tree. Icicles cut from silver tea packages completed the effect. The setting sun shone brightly through the west windows as I worked, and the heat from the little room stove drew out the sweet woodsy odor from the tree.

As this was our first Christmas together, all our friends remembered us and we received a large number of cards. I had carefully hidden them in the cupboard as they arrived, to be taken out and re-read on Christmas Eve. As darkness fell, I lit the kerosene lamp and we read the story of the Savior's Birth from the Gospel. Our cards were brought out and we read them together, then my husband arranged them in a circle around the base of the tree. They were all lovely, but one card was especially beautiful. It pictured three wise men on camels journeying to a little town far in the distance and overhead, leading ever onward, shone the star. With a heart full of happiness and thanks to God, I read the beautiful greeting:

> Dear Wilson and Bertha,
> May the Star that led the wise men
> To the humble manger bed
> Shine out for you and lead you too
> Through all the days ahead.

[Published in *The Recaller*, November 1993. From *Through All the Days Gone By*, Bertha Mae MacIntyre MacDonald. Reprinted with permission from Pearle McKenna.]

# Memories of Christmas Past

**Robert Ross** "I got a truck one time – it was fairly big, and that's the only toy I remember."

**Joyce Kennedy** "Books – I loved to get a book."

**Hesta MacDonald** "When my oldest brother got a job in the bank, he gave me an Eaton's Beauty Doll, and I still have it."

**Kathleen Ross** "I remember one year Mom got ski caps for me and my sister. She hid them under the cushions of the chesterfield, and we found them there. Every day we'd try them on, and I used to wonder which one was going to be for me. They had little flaps that came down, and I'd pull on those. By the time Christmas came, we had them almost worn out."

**Jessie MacKinnon** "I will always remember Roddie and Marion MacKenzie who came to my parents home on Christmas Eve with a basket filled with cookies, candy and fruit. They had no family of their own, but always remembered the neighbor families."

[Published in *The Recaller*, November 1993.]

**Old Fashioned Christmas Post Card.** [Courtesy of Auldene MacKenzie.]

# The Hunters and the Bear

*Lizzie MacIntosh of Belle River*
February 8, 1902

The winter set in quietly along Belle River shore
And everything was silent except the loud wind's roar.
From many a cozy dwelling were smoke wreaths curling high
And heavy snow clouds drifted against a frowning sky.

The girls were hooking, quilting, and casting many a gaze
Out over the bleak, bare landscape and longed for warmer days.
The farmers smoked and chatted; the women knit and spun
The boys were growing restless for want of sport and fun.

One night in cold December, excitement filled the air
For back of Allan Matheson's, Sandy Ronald saw a bear.
The news went flying widespread, as only news can do,
And many a skeptic whispered, "Do you suppose it's true?"

But, the old men answered quietly, "Sandy Ronald ought to know,
For he has met with many bears in New Brunswick long ago."
Then all the women shuddered, the girls said, "I declare!"
But the boys were just delighted, a treat like this was rare.

So every jolly fellow went home to clean his gun
And when some snow had fallen, the hunting was begun.
But many a frosty evening the hunters homeward came
With frozen ears and fingers, but nothing of their game.

Then Stewart, Bill and Hector and many a curious chap
Who prowled the tangled woodland, roused Bruin from his nap.
The sound of reckless shooting passed through his hidden lair
And a most disgusted fellow was that old sleepy bear.

"A gang of merry hunters, and armed with muskets stout.
I guess I'll leave Belle River before they shoot me out.
Oh yes, I'll go some morning when snow is falling fast
And the hunters all are indoors, protected from the blast."

One day two little urchins enjoyed a pleasant romp
Until they spied Old Bruin in MacIntosh's swamp.
The shaggy creature vanished, to Frankie's great surprise,
Among some nearby bushes, before his wondering eyes.

That night, when darkness covered this peaceful, quiet land,
The bear went struggling forward and reached Belle River's strand.
He stopped to watch the lamp lights that shone upon the snow,
And said, "I like Belle River, but still I've got to go.

Young hunters love your country, and take a bear's advice,
I'm off for Nova Scotia across the shining ice.
I've roughed it many a winter, men chased me here and there,
But still they'll do some hunting before they catch this bear."

So, here's to Mr. Bruin, I hope he's snug and warm
And sleeping most contented, while howls the winter storm.
And when the spring-time visits this land and Bruin's here,
May it bring joy and gladness to the hunter and the bear.

[Published in *The Recaller*, September 1985.]

## Chapter Eleven

❧

# The Belfast Historical Society Recalling Our Past...

**Ensignia of the Belfast Historical Society designed by the Prince Edward Island Heritage Foundation's Alan Rankin especially for the Founding Meeting of the society on March 26, 1976.**

# Founding of the Belfast Historical Society

*Harry Baglole*

The Belfast Historical Society was officially founded at a public meeting held on March 26, 1976.

The idea of forming a local historical society grew out of an Island History Course held in 1975 at the Belfast Community School. A committee of interested persons took on the task of drawing up a draft Constitution and calling a public meeting.

The principle objective of the Belfast Historical Society is to promote and encourage an interest in the history of the Belfast District.

Meetings and Society sponsored lectures are held several times during the year. During the first year, the Society sponsored three well-attended public lectures on local and Island history.

A founding member, Annie MacMillan of Wood Islands. For over ten years Annie served as Treasurer on the Executive Committee. [Photo courtesy of Ruth Acorn.]

The idea of a community historical society was new in Prince Edward Island when the Belfast Historical Society was first formed. We hope that our Society has been successful enough that other Island communities will want to follow our example.

The members of the first Executive Committee of the Belfast Historical Society were: Grace MacLeod, Point Prim; Janet Dale, Orwell Cove; Annie MacMillan, Wood Islands; Mary MacEachern, Garfield; Hugh MacDonald, Pinette; Ross MacPherson, Eldon; Dan Compton, Belle River; Mike O'Brien, Iona; and Harry Baglole, Mount Buchanan.

[Published in *The Recaller*, Autumn 1976.]

# The Belfast Historical Society Objectives

The Belfast Historical Society is a volunteer, registered charitable organization with membership open to anyone with an interest in Island life and Belfast community history.

The general objectives of the society are defined in the Society Constitution as:

1. To promote and encourage an interest in the history of the Belfast District.

2. To identify, collect, and preserve historic documents, artifacts, and information of local interest and significance.

3. To cooperate with the Prince Edward Island Heritage Foundation in collecting and preserving materials of province-wide interest.

The specific objectives of the society are defined in the Society Constitution as:

1. To do research into the history of the Belfast District, and to share the findings of this research through the publication of pamphlets, books, a regular newsletter to be sent to members of the Society, and by other appropriate means.

2. To hold at least six general meetings of the Society each year, at each of which there shall be some program, such as a guest speaker or a discussion of the history of the local area.

3. To encourage in young people, by cooperation with schools and other means, an interest in the history of the local area.

4. To gather and record unwritten stories and information that exist only in the memories of the older people.

5. To commemorate historic events by appropriate ceremonies.

6. To mark in a suitable manner sites of historic interest, or to make recommendations to proper authority respecting the marketing of the same.

7. To work toward a local museum which will house objects and documents collected.

# The Belfast Historical Society Executive

## 1976/77
President Harry Baglole; Vice President Grace MacLeod; Treasurer Annie MacMillan; Secretary Janet Dale; Directors Daniel Compton, Hugh MacDonald, Mary MacEachern, Ross MacPherson, and Mike O'Brien; Recaller Editor Mary Ross.

## 1977/78
President Harry Baglole; Vice President Daniel Compton; Treasurer Annie MacMillan; Secretary Keith MacPherson; Directors Hugh MacDonald, Mary MacEachern, Angus McGowan, Grace MacLeod, and Ross MacPherson; Recaller Editor Mary Ross.

## 1978/79
President Mary Ross; Vice President Daniel Compton; Treasurer Annie MacMillan; Secretary and Past President Harry Baglole; Directors Mary MacEachern, Alan MacKenzie, Keith MacPherson, and Ross MacPherson; Recaller Editor Mary Ross

## 1979/80
President Mary Ross; Vice President Daniel Compton; Treasurer Annie MacMillan; Secretary Harry Baglole; Directors Mary MacEachern, Angus McGowan, Donald MacKenzie, Mrs. Reginald Smith, and Canon Robert C. Tuck; Recaller Editor Mary Ross

## 1980/81
President Mary Ross; Vice President Donald MacKenzie; Treasurer Annie MacMillan; Secretary Harry Baglole; Directors Daniel Compton, Mary MacEachern, Angus McGowan, Jean MacKenzie, and Margaret Smith; Recaller Editor Mary Ross.

## 1981/82
Same as previous year, except new Director Boyd Livingstone.

## 1982/83
Same as previous year, except new Directors Donald MacDonald and Ross MacPherson and new Recaller Editor Hesta MacDonald.

## 1983/84
President Hesta MacDonald; Past President Mary Ross; Vice President Donald MacKenzie; Treasurer Annie MacMillan; Secretary Jean MacKenzie; Directors Harry Baglole, Daniel Compton, Mary Cook, Boyd Livingstone, Mary MacEachern, Angus McGowan, Ross MacPherson, and Margaret Smith; Recaller Editor Hesta MacDonald.

## 1984/85
Same as previous year, except new Directors Alan Buchanan and John MacKinnon replaced Boyd Livingstone and Mary MacEachern, and returning Recaller Editor Mary Ross.

## 1985/86
President Hesta MacDonald; Vice President Alan Buchanan; Treasurer Annie MacMillan; Secretary Jean MacKenzie; Directors Harry Baglole, Daniel Compton, Mary Cook, Angus McGowan, Donald MacKenzie, John MacKinnon, Ross MacPherson, and Margaret Smith.; Recaller Editor Mary McGowan.

## 1986/87
Same as previous year, except new Directors Mary Ross and Ruby MacWilliams replaced Mary Cook, Harry Baglole, and Daniel Compton.

## 1987/88

Same as previous year.

## 1988/89

Same as previous year, except new Director James Halliday.

## 1989/90

President Alan Buchanan; Past President Hesta MacDonald; Vice President James Halliday; Treasurer Eliza Gillis; Secretary Jean MacKenzie; Directors Margaret Smith, Ross MacPherson, Mary Ross, Donald MacKenzie, and Kenneth MacKenzie; Recaller Editor Hesta MacDonald; Cards Olive Nicholson.

## 1990/91

Same as previous year except Margaret Smith was no longer a Director.

## 1991/92

President Alan Buchanan; Vice President James Halliday; Treasurer Eliza Gillis; Secretary Joyce Kennedy; Directors Kenneth MacDonald, Donald MacKenzie, Jean MacKenzie, William Stewart, and Mary Ross; Recaller Editor Hesta MacDonald.

## 1992/93

Same as previous year.

## 1993/94

President Thelma MacTavish; Past President Alan Buchanan; Vice President James Halliday; Treasurer Eliza Gillis; Secretary Joyce Kennedy; Directors William Stewart, Mary Ross, Donald MacKenzie, Jean MacKenzie, and Kenneth MacDonald; Recaller Editor Hesta MacDonald.

## 1994/95

President Alan Buchanan; Past President Thelma MacTavish; Vice President Annabelle Brehaut; Treasurer Eliza Gillis; Secretary Joyce Kennedy; Directors William Stewart, Mary Ross, Donald MacKenzie, Jean MacKenzie, and Kenneth MacDonald; Recaller Editor Hesta MacDonald.

## 1995/96

President Alan Buchanan; Vice President James Halliday; Treasurer Eliza Gillis; Secretary Joyce Kennedy; Directors Viola Gillis, Gordon MacEachern, Jean MacKay, Ernest MacLeod, John MacRae, and Sinclair MacTavish; Recaller Editor Hesta MacDonald.

## 1996/97

Same as previous year.

## 1997/98

President Dr. Jean Halliday MacKay; Vice President James Halliday; Treasurer Rebecca Matheson; Secretary Joyce Kennedy; Directors Donald MacKenzie, Mary Ross, William Stewart, Eliza Gillis, Alan Buchanan, Viola Gillis, and Jean Cantelo; Recaller Editor Hesta MacDonald.

## 1998/99

Same as previous year.

## 1998/99

President Hesta MacDonald; Vice President Dr. Jean Halliday MacKay; Treasurer Eliza Gillis, Secretary Joyce Kennedy; Directors Jean Cantelo, Viola Gillis, Donald MacKenzie, Rebecca Matheson, Dr. Mary Ross, and William Stewart; Recaller Editor Hesta MacDonald.

## 1999/2000

Same as previous year.

## 2000/01

Same as previous year except new Director Billy Cook and new Recaller Editor Linda J. Nicholson MacKenzie.

## 2001/2002

Same as previous year.

---

# Highlights of the Past Twenty-Five Years

**March 26, 1976**  The Founding Meeting of the Belfast Historical Society was held at the Belfast Consolidated School.  Chairman Waldo Taylor called the meeting to order and Rev. Gillis opened the meeting with a prayer.  The Constitution of the Society was adopted and the first Executive Committee elected.  Guest Speaker for the evening was the Hon. J. Angus MacLean.

**November 1976**  Editor Mary Ross mailed the first issue of the Belfast Historical Society newsletter to over 90 Society members.  The name initially suggested for the newsletter was *The Belfast Riot*, but the Executive Committee opted for *The Recaller*, a less controversial title.

**February 4, 1977**  The Executive Committee discussed applying for funding to offset the costs of compiling an oral history of Belfast.  In May, a grant was received and the work began.

**May 1977**  The first Dr. Angus MacAulay History Awards were presented to students for excellence in local history projects.

**December 1978**  The first Lord Selkirk Awards were presented to local residents Arthur Cantelo and John MacPherson.

**July 1981**  At the suggestion of Margaret Smith, the Belfast Historical Society hosted a Tea at St. John's Church.  Reminiscent of earlier "Belfast Teas" which were held in Belfast a century before, the tea was well attended.  It was decided this should be an annual event.

**September 24, 1987**  Based on the soon to be published *Belfast People*, a play dramatizing the lives of several Belfast area residents opened at the David MacKenzie Theatre in Charlottetown.

**February 17, 1992**  The Belfast Historical Society received the prestigious "Canadian Parks Service Heritage Award" in recognition of their efforts to preserve and interpret the history of the Belfast area.

**August 10, 1992**  The Belfast Historical Society launches the long awaited oral history *Belfast People*.  Initially called *Wait Till I Tell Ya*, this long awaited book was very well received.

**June 21, 1993**  The Belfast Historical Society is presented with a Publishing Award from the Prince Edward Island Museum and Heritage Foundation for *Belfast People*.

---

**Island stone with plaque in Penny's field.** [Photo courtesy of L. J. N. MacKenzie.]

**July 18, 1988** A service was held to dedicate a plaque to mount on a memorial stone in the grove at Penny's field. The plaque commemorates the unmarked burial place of some early settlers, most with the surnames Halliday and Larrabee.

**Belfast Historical Society President Hesta MacDonald. Hesta has been actively involved in the Society for 20 years.**

**August 26, 2000** More than 200 people attended a ceremony to commemorate the restoration of St. Paul's Ancient Cemetery. The celebration was a blend of both Acadian and Scottish culture. The highlight of the day was the unveiling of a commemorative plaque situated at the entrance to the cemetery.

The Belfast Historical Society had undertaken the project of restoring the cemetery. As part of this project, the Belle River Church of Scotland (built in 1876) was purchased by the Society and moved to a site across from the cemetery.

# History of the Selkirk Awards

*Joyce Kennedy*

At the May 1978 meeting of the Belfast Historical Society, President Mary Ross suggested the Society establish special awards to recognize adults who, through research or study, contributed to Belfast Community History. Similar to the Dr. Angus MacAulay Awards, this award would be given for a wide range of projects.

The membership approved a motion to establish the new awards, to be named "The Selkirk Awards" in honour of Thomas Douglas, the Fifth Earl of Selkirk, and a committee was formed to establish guidelines.

It was determined that "The Selkirk Awards" were to be given annually to individuals or groups in recognition of excellence for projects undertaken on the history of the Belfast district, or for outstanding contributions to preserving the heritage of the Belfast area. Recipients of this award would be presented with an engraved plaque.

To date, recipients of this award include:

**1979**
*Arthur Cantelo* for his replica of St. John's Church.
*John MacPherson*, operator of the only remaining Island sawmill run by water-power.

**1980**
*Wood Islands Women's Institute* for their hooked rug depicting community life.
*Kenneth and Shelly MacKenzie* for the restoration of their Eldon home.
*Eleanor Gillis* for her historical paintings of Point Prim.

**1981**
*Johnny Panton* for restoration work in St. John's Presbyterian Church Cemetery.

**1982**
*George Young* and *Angus McGowan* for their contributions to the oral history of Belfast.

**1983**
*Edgar Munn* for his interest in the preservation of community history.

**1984**
*Mary Ross* for her efforts in promoting interest in local history.

**1989**
*Hesta MacDonald* for her contribution to the preservation of the heritage of Belfast.

**1999**
*Jean Cantelo* for restoration work on her historic house.

**2001**
*Donald Garnhum*, *Ernest MacLeod*, and *William Stewart* for their part in preserving our heritage.

**2002**
*Isabel MacDonald* for her contribution to the preservation of the heritage of Belfast.

# MacAulay Awards

The MacAulay Awards were named for Dr. Angus MacAulay, a principal agent for Lord Selkirk, who brought settlers from Scotland to the Belfast area in 1803. These awards are given by the Belfast Historical Society to school children for their work on local history projects.

**1977**
David Gamble

**1978**
Paul Larsen
Susan MacRae
Mark Mooney
John McCabe

**1979**
Natalie Bears

**1980**
Bonnie Jean McCabe
Dawn Kerr
Sheila Bell

**1981**
Kimberly MacKinnon

**1982**
Rhonda Ann McCabe
Eileen MacMillan
Shawn MacKenzie

**1985**
Bradley Davies
George Duncan

**1986**
Richard Lynch
Shawn Kerr

**1987**
Julie Anne Gillis
Robyn Murchison

**1988**
Darcy McCabe
Jason Docherty
Laura McBurnie

**1989**
Kendall Docherty
Deborah Jean Cooper
Garth Nicholson

**1990**
Robbie Johnston
Amanda MacLeod
Ian Murray

**1991**
B. J. Stewart
Marsha Knox
Janie Gillis

**1992**
Andrew MacPhee
Kenda Lee McCabe
Jackie Roche

**1994**
Erin MacDonald
D. J. Albrecht
Mark MacKenzie
Honorable mention –
Melissa Henry

**1995**
Matthew Gillis
Troy MacLean
Rebecca Halliday

**1996**
Kyle MacMillan
Devin McCabe

**1998**
Colin Buchanan
James MacPhee

# Editors

**Editors Viola Gillis, Linda J. N. MacKenzie, and Eliza Gillis.**
[Photo courtesy of Donna Collings.]

## Viola Gillis

Born in Wood Islands, Viola Gillis (nee MacDonald) moved to a farm in Lower Newtown when she married in 1962. Now a retired teacher, counselor and bookkeeper, she is involved in numerous organizations including the Belfast Historical Society. She enjoys family gatherings, reading, camping, travel and volunteer work.

## Linda Jean Nicholson MacKenzie

Born "away", but with Island roots, Linda MacKenzie moved to Belfast when she married in 1999. She is an accountant by profession, but for the past twenty years her main interest has been genealogy. She is active in several societies and is past Editor of the Belfast Historical Society newsletter.

## Eliza Gillis

Born in Mount Buchanan, Eliza Gillis (nee Morrison) has always lived in Belfast. She is a homemaker and part-time teacher. Now retired, she enjoys her grandchildren, gardening, reading and volunteering in her community. She has served on the Executive Committee of the Belfast Historical Society for over ten years.

# Index